QUIT ANXIETY NOW

With Smart Therapy™

Dr Sallee McLaren, clinical psychologist and director of the Smart Therapy centre clinic in Melbourne, Australia, has over two decades of experience helping thousands of anxious and distressed people recover without medication. With a background in brain research she has brought her extensive neurological knowledge into her daily clinical practice and has developed her own unique ST model and method of treatment. She is the author of *Don't Panic: You Can Overcome Anxiety Without Drugs*, and has recently developed an app called 'Smart Therapy' for use with mobile platforms.

Also by Dr Sallee McLaren

Don't Panic: You Can Overcome Anxiety Without Drugs (Scribe, 2004)

QUIT ANXIETY NOW

With Smart Therapy™

DR SALLEE MCLAREN

MUTATA PRESS

© Sallee McLaren 2017

First published 2017 by Mutata Press
and distributed by

Australian Scholarly Publishing Pty Ltd
7 Lt Lothian St Nth, North Melbourne, Vic 3051
Tel: 03 9329 6963 / Fax: 03 9329 5452
enquiry@scholarly.info / www.scholarly.info

ISBN 978-1-925588-35-4

ALL RIGHTS RESERVED

Cover design Wayne Saunders

PREFACE

This book can get you better. It is the book that anxious people all over the world have needed for a long time.

- The Smart Therapy method is simple and easy to follow.
- It can start working immediately.
- Once you understand it, it requires no real effort – it is enjoyable.
- It can work no matter how bad your symptoms are.
- You can get better permanently, without medication.
- Your life can transform from destructive to highly productive.
- There are no tricks or gimmicks – Smart Therapy is based on hard neuroscience.

Don't delay any longer, read this book – *your life and happiness may depend upon it!*

Please note that it is important to read the whole of this guide book before you start applying the method.

CONTENTS

**Part One:
What is the Basis of Smart Therapy?**

    An Overview of Smart Therapy...3

    1. Why Should I Try Smart Therapy?..8

    2. What Happens in Our Brains? 18

    3. You Are the Boss of Your Brain..40

**Part Two:
What is the Method of Smart Therapy?**

    4. Step One: Keep Your Behaviours Useful,
       Effective and Never Self-Sabotaging 63

    5. Step Two: Keep Yourself Relaxed
       and Always Below 3/10 74

    6. Step Three: Never Allow Yourself to Pay Attention to
       Even a Single Self-Sabotaging Mentation *Ever Again*!..........94

    7. Step Four: Keep Shifting Your Attention
       100% Onto Constructive Activities 112

Part Three:
How Do I Use Smart Therapy in Practice?

8. Geraldine's Story:
   Straight-Forward Anxiety 127

9. Daniel's Story: Complex Anxiety
   and Other Difficulties 144

Part Four:
How Do I Make My Smart Therapy Improvements Permanent?

10. Ensuring You Never Go Back There 183

Appendix:
The Neurological Basis of Smart Therapy 205

References 230

PART ONE:

WHAT IS THE BASIS OF SMART THERAPY?

AN OVERVIEW OF SMART THERAPY

Smart Therapy (ST) is a completely new, revolutionary and unique approach to anxiety. Unlike all other current treatments within the mental health system, ST identifies anxiety as simply a *habit* that is learned no differently to every other form of learning. Getting over anxiety is as simple as learning to stop paying attention to it – and this short guide will show you exactly how to do this so you can be forever free from its grip.

Increasingly, and for too long, anxiety has been identified as a biochemical imbalance that is either genetic in origin or pathological or both. Anxiety problems are defined as 'disorders' within all the main treatment manuals that mental health professionals use for diagnosis. Many mental health professionals then further entrench this perception by encouraging the use of medication to 'alleviate the disorder'.

Once diagnosed and entrenched, these problems can easily become part of peoples' identity whereby they perceive themselves as 'anxious' and believe anxiety to be an intrinsic part of their personality that cannot be changed and which therefore *requires* ongoing medication and professional intervention.

This is simply inaccurate and untrue. There is a much simpler and far more compelling explanation for why people become anxious and that explanation shows us very clearly exactly how we can transcend it permanently, going on to have constructive, self-reflective, meaningful, happy and fulfilled lives.

WHAT I NOTICED INITIALLY

Very soon after starting work more than two decades ago as a clinical psychologist, I noticed that many treatment approaches simply didn't work or made anxious people worse. In particular, I noticed that people who were taking medications, like antidepressants, although they often *initially* felt better (possibly due to the 'placebo' effect), in the long-run they were unlikely to recover – whereas people who were not taking medications generally *did* recover, even if their symptoms were much worse to begin with. This led me to write a book called *Don't Panic: You Can Overcome Anxiety Without Drugs* in 2004.

I also noticed very early on that one of the main treatment approaches, called Cognitive Behavioural Therapy (CBT), was very uneven in its results. In particular, people became worse when they were encouraged to mentally explore and challenge their anxious thoughts. On the other hand, when behavioural interventions were put in place they tended to get better. So I started trying to work out why this might be the case.

As it happened I had a research background and strong interest in brain research (albeit with chickens and rats!) and my past work had a particular focus on the physiology of learning and memory. Over the years, my constant exploration of the latest neurological research provided me with the basis to gradually develop the ST theory and to observe my clients and furnish them with ever-more precise practical interventions to establish what worked quickly and effectively for all types of anxiety and for many other problems as well.

Even though it might initially seem strange to claim to have a solution to all types of anxiety, it is actually quite logical. As you would know, every brain is different because each brain is developed from a specific set of circumstances and contexts. No two people have exactly the same environment or experiences (not even identical twins). Since we all build our brains precisely in response to our individual environmental experience, each of our brains is different in terms of content. So how can one solution work for all of these different brains?

Well, the crucial point here is that although the specific information held within each brain is different, the way our brains work and lay down that information is essentially the same. Physiologically, we all learn, consolidate and retrieve material from memory in *exactly* the same way.

In order to develop the ST theory I had to step outside the way 'mental illness' was perceived as an *individual defect* by almost everyone. I asked myself 'what if all these different types of anxiety are not pathologies at all but simply reflect *normal* learning and memory processes?' After all, I knew from neurological research that despite massive research efforts, no biochemical imbalance or genetic pathology had ever been conclusively demonstrated or extrapolated to population samples in the brains of anxious people.

On the other hand, what I did notice in my anxiety clinic, without exception, in *every* single person that I ever saw (and there were thousands of them) was that they all had one thing in common: They were all **worrying** and, in worrying they were focusing their attention intensely on their anxious and self-sabotaging ruminations. In other words, everyone who came to my clinic for help was *paying attention* to their distress. They were going over and over their fearful and distressing thoughts, usually for many hours every day.

As it happened, I knew from my past research in learning and memory that a very large number of robust studies over long periods of time had consistently demonstrated that what we pay attention to, *we learn*. Indeed, paying attention is the precise way we make our brains distinguish between important and unimportant material in our environment. That is, we pay attention to what we think is important and we don't bother to pay attention to what is not important.

Moreover, in the learning process of repetitively paying attention, we consolidate the targeted material into long-term memory (LTM). Once in long-term memory we can retrieve the targeted material easily and, if we do so frequently, we will increasingly consolidate it whereby it becomes a larger and larger part of our subjective experience simply by paying attention to it ever more often.

Back in 2004 when I wrote my first book, no-one, including myself, knew for sure how paying attention led to learning and memory consolidation at a neurological level but we knew it did happen, so in my book although I strongly discouraged people from paying attention to their ruminations the exact mechanisms for *why* that was the case were not yet known.

Also, at the time there was very little cross-over of any neurological knowledge into the clinical setting and almost all clinicians, in any case, were strongly locked into the 'disorder' and 'pathology' framework, seeing anxiety as a *defect* within the *individual*, not as a normal process. As a consequence most health professionals advocated clients delve extensively into their emotions, thoughts and memories and try to challenge and correct the 'defect'.

At that time and often still today, people with anxiety are encouraged to focus strongly on their fears to try to 'desensitise' themselves and professionals even make recordings of client fears so clients can replay and listen to their fears outside of session. For example, in Post-Traumatic Stress Disorder (PTSD) clients are frequently encouraged to delve into their terrifying memories of the traumatic event in an attempt to desensitise and reconfigure the event.

Back then, the dilemma for me was that although these were the established and recommended treatment approaches – I was observing every day in my clinic that paying ever more attention to the very difficulties most clients wanted to be rid of, **was just making people worse**. The more people paid attention to their fears and depressive ruminations the more they learned, remembered and retrieved them with ever-increasing frequency.

Fortunately, in the last decade there have been huge advances in microscopy technologies. These advances have enabled us to directly observe single neurons and even single synapses (brain connections between neurons). Nowadays we can also directly observe many of the exact physiological processes involved in learning and memory. As a result of these microscopy advances, I have finally been able to develop the finer points of the ST theory which is based on this directly-observed, cutting-edge neurological research.

Anyway, I hope you love ST. As its name reflects, ST will not cause emotional dependency or mind-numbing effects like medications. Instead, ST is all about harnessing our 'smarts' and applying our extraordinary human brain power to ensure permanent and comprehensive self-rescue!

CHAPTER ONE
WHY SHOULD I TRY SMART THERAPY?

The main reason you should try ST is because it works! The reason I am so confident ST is highly effective is not just because it has worked with thousands of my clients (although that obviously helps!) but because it worked so remarkably for me. I was a person who came from a difficult background that resulted in many messed-up ways of dealing with life. I left home at 16 years, working at night to support myself at school during the day. In my final year of secondary school my marks were pretty dismal and I was going nowhere except to work in a large psychiatric hospital – an institution that perpetuated much of the brutality I was already used to.

By the time I reached my early adulthood and after many dead-end jobs I was distraught: highly anxious and panicking, depressed (with a bleak and flat mood of around 1–2/10), relentlessly anticipating every possible catastrophe, over-worrying for hours every day and constantly thinking of ways to die. I was experiencing terrifying repetitive nightmares and flashbacks, I was angry, paranoid, addicted, under-weight or over-weight, moving from relationship to relationship, and suffering from intractable insomnia! I even heard voices. I was utterly miserable, lost, despairing and angry about it – in turn, blaming others, being hostile, feeling powerless, collapsing and crying, screaming, demanding, over-eating then starving myself while smoking and drinking myself towards oblivion.

Although that was a desolate time, it taught me many valuable lessons that eventually led me to enrol at university and study to become first a registered nurse and then later a clinical psychologist. One benefit of my miserable life was that it drove me on in my work as a clinical psychologist to find *real* solutions that *genuinely work*. Also, it helped me to work fairly effortlessly with all my clients, because pretty much no matter what they came in with, I had had the same thing usually many times worse in my own early life! That meant I could tell them exactly how to get rid of almost any problem!

Nowadays, and for the past 25 years I have had a buoyant, stable and happy mood of around 8/10, been relaxed, calm, productive, engaged in many interests and hobbies, non-addicted to *any* substance, of average Body Mass Index, extremely happily married, engaged in a stable career, non-obsessed, free from repetitive nightmares or flashbacks, completely uninterested in ways to die, and generally sleeping well. I no longer hear voices. Yet in my early adulthood I never thought I would be able to get myself out of the deep hole I was in – a vicious cycle of unrelenting anxiety, lowered mood, anger, paranoia and self-sabotage which made me feel powerless and unable to act on my own behalf and break out of it. Yet I did – and I did so using ST (although it did not have its name then): a simple, easy and painless approach, no medications or side-effects, just a *simple mental shift*.

OUR AILING MENTAL HEALTH SYSTEM AND BIG PHARMA

Despite the ease of the ST solution it has been remarkably difficult to get the message out there into the mainstream. There is a clear resistance from many mental health professionals to methods that are quick, preventative and permanent. It was about twenty years ago that I started trying to get ST into the mainstream. Back then, I used to say things to my husband like:

'We have got this *so terribly* wrong – drug companies, psychiatrists and many mental health workers have got a lot to answer for! So many people put on huge doses of medications, making them unable to think clearly or defend their own interests properly. The revolving door of psychiatric units and the constant stigma, debasement and pathology of diagnosis – surely we can do better than this – the mental health system really is a public disgrace!'

Still, decades later, the ailing mental health system limps onwards – indeed it is growing by exponential tax dollars each year. The mainstream mental health agencies continue, unabated in their medication and revolving-door approach to what is, in my view, mostly just *normal* human distress that could be quickly and effectively corrected – yet it is currently managed very poorly indeed.

This is partly of course, because large pharmaceutical companies (also known as 'Big Pharma') are a multi-trillion-dollar industry, which are primarily focussed on *alleviating* symptoms – not preventing them and not getting people over them. Big Pharma is penetrating almost every sphere of our society worldwide largely under the banner of 'medical science' and about a quarter of the population is now 'medicated' in most Western countries. Big Pharma has managed this despite achieving (at best) consistently poor to mediocre outcomes in published drug trial studies and, close examination of many of their studies show that they only manage to achieve their fairly dismal results by frequently 'dropping out' research subjects who experience debilitating side-effects. On the other hand, there are numerous drug trial studies that never even get published because their outcomes are, well, so bad they are unpublishable!

The diseased mental health system also keeps going because many mental health professionals are, to varying extents caught up in the financial merry-go-round of Big Pharma, especially those who prescribe their drugs and receive other *informal* benefits such as career advancement, gifts and holidays for lending their endorsement to Big Pharma products.

There are also though, the financial incentives that operate on professionals to keep people 'mentally ill'. For example, psychiatrists get excessively large government rebates for patient sessions and the longer the patient remains 'ill' the more payments are received. Not only this, but the excessive government payments are given for very brief sessions (about enough time to write a prescription rather than deliver anything of substance in terms of strategies for recovery).

Psychologists are also caught up in the system but to a lesser extent as they receive very limited government payments and at least, have to put in extensive time to strategise with their clients without bombing them into oblivion with medications. But nonetheless, they have become part of the larger mental health machine and with it many psychologists have also embraced the ideology of 'pathology'.

Which brings me to, by far, the biggest problem that allows the deplorable mental health system to keep going and that is the *ideology* underlying it which is largely unquestioned and therefore passively supported by most people in our society, thereby allowing it to continue.

AN INACCURATE IDEOLOGY UNDERLIES AND JUSTIFIES OUR SICK MENTAL HEALTH SYSTEM

The ideology that underlies, perpetuates and justifies our deeply troubled mental health system arises originally from *biological determinism* which assumes *individual pathology* from the outset before considering other (often more likely) causes *outside* the individual (like environmental stress).

If we start from the assumption of individual pathology and deficiency then the next rational step allows people to be diagnosed as 'mentally ill' by having so-called mental 'disorders' or mental deficiencies. Mental health 'bibles' like the current DSM-V that list hundreds of 'disorders' are immediately justified under this ideology.

In my view, this is an enormous travesty of human justice as many of the so-called 'disorders' are actually just *normal* human distress that, if handled correctly can often be efficiently and quickly fixed up (more on this soon). On the other hand, notions of 'mental disorder' are able to rationalise the whole medical/psychiatric machinery intrinsic to the mental health system and provide justification for interventions like medication, incarceration, electroconvulsive therapy (ECT), neuro-surgery and the like.

One of the events that helped me to start to think differently about 'mental health' happened when I was an 'intern' in a large public hospital and I came up against two psychiatrists who were advocating major neuro-surgery for a young woman who was anxious and suffering from severe 'obsessive compulsive disorder' (more widely known as 'OCD'). So zealous was their approach that they were advocating major brain surgery without even attempting to help her with simple behavioural interventions first!

At the time, I was completely shocked. I argued with them about their course of action, while about twenty other health professionals in the room remained completely silent – they were probably horrified at me objecting so stridently! In any case, I insisted on working with the anxious woman before any surgery was carried out. Unable to properly defend their case, the psychiatrists eventually and reluctantly gave me two weeks to get her better.

At the time, I was only a student and not well-skilled in the area, but I applied myself to the task as best I could at the time, and even with only two weeks of intervention she improved (about 85% of her 'symptoms' went away) and the surgery was not performed.

That experience taught me some of the dangers of the mental health system, and why it is best wherever possible to stay well away from it. Nowadays with the precision of the ST approach, I know that even extremely severe 'OCD' can almost always be resolved super-fast and with no risk of the side-effects of either medication or surgery!

Despite this, the enormous and dysfunctional mental health machine persists in its daily devastation, since the financial returns are so compelling and the underlying ideology remains largely unquestioned. Also, people who are distressed and demoralised are very easy targets. In fact, the mental health system kind of *requires* a certain level of *passivity*, where health professionals expect patients to just passively pop a pill and go to hospital and receive their ECT without question, rather than actively seeking out better and more permanent and preventative solutions.

WE CAN DO THIS BETTER AND SMART THERAPY IS ONE WAY TO DO IT

Luckily for me when I was anxious and distressed in my own life, I had two things going for me. Firstly, I was frightened of incarceration, so I avoided psychiatrists and medication like the plague, and secondly, I wasn't passive about asking questions! When something I tried didn't work I wanted to know why and when something did work I equally made it my business to understand the reasons.

In my studies and later my clinical work, bit by bit, I unravelled clues which led me to develop a theory and then to continuously return to the empirical literature to examine the latest neurological findings. I was constantly back and forth testing out behavioural interventions on myself and my clients to see what led to recovery and what did not.

In the next chapter I will give you some detail about that empirical literature and what happens neurologically when we pay attention and I will also talk about how these neurological processes can be manipulated by all of us to get over anxiety (and many other difficulties) permanently.

But first, I will explain a few more things about ST. Above all, ST is incredibly *easy* to do. For me, and for my clients who have successfully applied ST, this was a major surprise! It was not just easy but enjoyable!

Given that anxiety has always been regarded as 'intrinsic' and part of the very fabric of an individual, getting rid of it has been (wrongly) regarded as very complex and tantamount to climbing Mount Everest. This is an absolute myth!

In reality it is amazingly easy to get over anxiety so long as you know exactly what you have to do. I will, of course give you more detail on this later on, but essentially you just have to understand that all your anxiety is no more than a *habit* to be relinquished and therefore you need pay it no further attention.

When I decided to 'give up' and 'quit' my bad habit of paying attention to unwanted and useless anxiety thoughts, feelings, memories, images or sensations, it was actually such a relief!

I no longer had to worry myself sick for hours on end every day: scaring myself stupid by anticipating the worst, then planning my responses or 'solutions' to the worst, then worrying and self-doubting that I would be ineffectual in my responses, making me anticipate other worse-case scenarios and so on.

Once I quit, I no longer had the constant day-in, day-out worrying which led me to become completely demoralised, so that I smoked or drank large amounts giving myself addiction problems, or alternatively, over-ate food to try to make myself feel better, especially comfort foods like bread, chips, lollies or chocolate. It was so great to then be able to stop putting myself through punishing starvation and exercise regimes to try and undo the damage of my indulgences!

Once I made a full commitment to stop paying attention to my useless mental habits, I was suddenly liberated from my own prison. It was such a relief not to have to examine and scrutinise anxious, depressive, morbid and self-sabotaging thoughts. I was **free**! Free from my vicious and exhausting cycles of relentless self-sabotage. All I had to do was engage in constructive activities all day long – activities that advanced and progressed me! Activities I enjoyed and loved!

Instead of worrying and obsessing I could happily read the newspaper, I could knock myself out doing crosswords or Sudoku puzzles, I could get totally absorbed in my latest novel. Alternatively, I could enjoy watching documentaries on TV, go for runs and bike rides, study fascinating material, go for rock-climbs, listen to talk-back radio, play the flute, do work tasks, plan future constructive activities, sing, read journals or factual material, socialise, do yoga, engage in vigorous conversations, dance, have interesting discussions, do mathematics puzzles, enjoy intimacy, work hard in the garden, go to community events, take up hobbies (like ceramics or cooking or dog training classes), do weights, play basketball, or get out in the beautiful sun and go for swims. Tough, heh?

All I had to do was just make sure that I did absolutely no worrying; no self-recrimination; no anxious, depressive or angry rumination; pay not a shred of attention to any anxious physiological feelings or sensations (like increased heart rate, sweats or nausea), shift my attention away from any unwanted mental images, and ensure that I did not engage in any thinking about addiction or self-sabotage. **In short, I could not focus on anything that I did not want to make a larger presence in my brain.**

On the other hand, I could think endlessly about anything that I *did* want to become a larger presence in my brain – so I often mentally worked out dance steps I was learning or thought about statistical problems I was solving or recalled facts that I was studying or imagined pieces of music I was learning or problem-solved clients' dilemmas or recalled rock-climbing techniques or sequences that I wanted to make sure I did not forget.

What I found, was that when I *decisively* stopped paying attention to all of those self-destructive, anxious and depressive thoughts that I used to spend hours every day thinking about, they became fewer and fewer *extremely* quickly. So quickly, in fact, that it was almost immediate! I was quite suddenly better – I had become a non-worrier within days! It was like flicking a switch.

With a shock, I realised that ST was not just a method to get over problems – it was the only *smart* method! I had found its name! I can tell you that ST worked for me so effortlessly and enjoyably, despite the fact that my dysfunction was considerably more extensive than many of the clients I currently see in my work. Back then, most people looking at me from the outside would have thought that I was damaged *to the core* – and I was! Yet a very simple, committed decision completely changed my life, and, given the severity of my dysfunction: **If I can do it, *anyone* can do it**!

CHAPTER TWO
WHAT HAPPENS IN OUR BRAINS?

I have made this chapter relatively straight-forward. If you would like more specific information about the current neuroscience and rationale that underpins ST then you can read a detailed, technical and referenced outline in the Appendix.

I have included this chapter because I find in my work that people do so much better and are far more motivated in getting over their difficulties if they understand a fair amount about what is actually happening in their brain at a neurological level.

This is probably because genuinely stopping paying attention requires strong commitment and increasing your knowledge base helps improve that commitment. So, please don't skip it! The difference might be decades or more of misery versus quickly achieving a constructive and enjoyable life.

DISTRESS IS NORMAL DURING DIFFICULT TIMES

When people go along to see mental health workers it is usually because they feel *distressed*. Most mental health workers describe this distress as being 'symptoms' but in this guide I am going to stick with the words 'distress' or 'brain agitation' and 'sensitisation' because these terms more accurately describe what is happening at both the psychological and neurological level.

The reason I do not use the word 'symptoms' (or other diagnostic terms except in inverted commas) is because I want to make it clear that this distress is actually completely *normal* in certain contexts and it does **not** arise from disease or pathology.

Before I go to the contexts of where it is normal to feel distress, let me just back up slightly and tell you exactly what I mean in this guide when I use these terms. 'Distress' describes a mental state where people (usually suddenly) feel unable to rest or calm-down, frequently finding it hard to sleep, eat or settle, feeling emotionally and physiologically disturbed, uneasy, tense, overwrought, full of dread and fragile. Often people lose their confidence and become afraid to trust their own judgement. This mental state of 'distress' arises from an increase in CRF (Corticotrophin Releasing Factor, more on this shortly) which causes 'brain agitation' and 'sensitisation' at a neural level.

At the time of the sudden onset of distress, people often feel more sensitive than usual and they can become hyper-vigilant and overly focused on particular mental themes. For example, some people might suddenly become convinced they have developed a life-threatening illness when, in reality, they are completely healthy. Other people might suddenly start to focus on depressive themes like their own failings or ways to self-harm even though their failings never overly concerned them in the past.

This state of distress is highly disturbing and unpleasant for people, who often believe they are actually going mad and that something is *seriously* wrong with them. This is why people often seek professional help at this time.

Interestingly, and as strange as it might seem, there is, almost certainly nothing pathologically wrong with these distressed people. In reality, what they are experiencing is a NORMAL response by the brain to an **abnormal** threat. It just feels very intense and overwhelming at the time.

WHAT IS THE ABNORMAL THREAT?

The threat is simply a stressful life event; and it is *normal* to feel distressed when and after we experience them. Within the scientific literature, it is now widely accepted that stressful life events have a clear, causative role in the onset of both anxiety and depressive 'symptoms'. It seems that anyone (even the most mentally robust individuals) will succumb to intense feelings of distress if the stressful life event is severe enough to warrant it.

Although stressful life events are normal (in that we *all* experience them) they are mostly *not* everyday events and are perceived by our brains as *abnormal*. Stressful life events tend to destabilise our sense of self. They include things like being retrenched from work, losing or separating from a partner, failing an important exam, experiencing severe and ongoing criticism, having a miscarriage, getting bullied, parental separation, migrating to another country, getting assaulted or becoming seriously ill.

We all have stressful life events, but most people, fortunately, do not have them too often. On the other hand, people who have come from *difficult backgrounds*, have experienced stressful life events more frequently compared to most people (that is the meaning of 'difficult background' in this book) and they have often felt ongoing distress for much of their lives.

Stressful life events almost always start anxiety and other forms of distress

STRESSFUL LIFE EVENTS THREATEN OUR 'SENSE OF SELF' OR IDENTITY

Stressful life events tend to shake and undermine our identity; that is, who we think we are and what our hopes for our own future might be. When solid expectations about ourselves are suddenly undermined, then we feel shocked and disorientated, and our brains respond by attempting to adapt to the threat.

This happens, for example, if we lose a job when we were expecting to have a successful career, or we miscarry a baby when we were expecting to become parents, or lose our life-partner when we were expecting to be together for many more years, or when we have our confidence in our own abilities undermined by ongoing harsh or brutal criticism, or if our parents separate when we assumed they would always stay together, or if we suddenly find that our life is going to be shorter or harder when we develop serious illness or disability. Basically, our hopes and expectations are dashed and we feel in danger and unsure of how to move forward.

So far, *every* anxious person that I have *ever* seen in my clinical practice experienced a stressful life event just prior to a noticeable and significant increase in mental distress, making it highly probable that stressful life events do lead to this brain agitation and sensitisation, and that it is not some individual defect, pathology or predisposition.

WHY DO STRESSFUL LIFE EVENTS CAUSE THIS INTERNAL AGITATION AND DISTRESS?

Every day, as a normal part of our functioning we all release a brain neuropeptide called Corticotrophin Releasing Factor (CRF) also known as Corticotrophin Releasing Hormone (CRH). Most CRF is released from the anterior pituitary gland (in the brain) and it regulates our daily bodily arousal state by activating many other hormones through the hypothalamic-pituitary-adrenal (HPA) axis.

However, when stressful life events happen our brains feel shocked and under *threat* and they respond by trying to adapt to the threat by producing *more* CRF than usual. Many replicated animal and human studies show this increase in CRF when chronic fear and threat are elicited under experimental conditions.

It is worth noting that in early human history, this CRF response occurred during long-term or chronic threats (like food or water shortage) and should not be confused with our fight and flight adrenaline response to immediate danger.

When we experience a stressful life event and CRF is released in much larger amounts, this does not only occur in the anterior pituitary gland and HPA axis, but we *additionally* release more CRF from other parts of the brain, in particular, from the amygdalae.

The amygdalae are part of the limbic system (the extremely old part of the brain often called the 'reptilian' brain), and they act as specialist areas that are responsible for detecting, processing and monitoring fear and threat. The amygdalae have high densities of CRF receptors that activate multiple neurotransmitter systems and communicate and relay signals to widespread and higher regions of the brain via the reticular formation and the thalamic pathways.

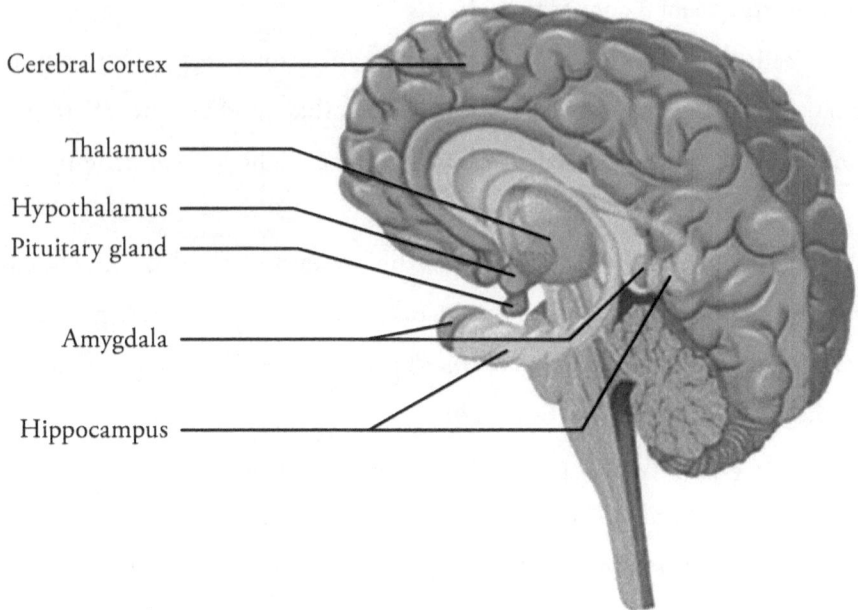

CRF is released from the pituitary and amygdala(e) during SLEs

CRF MAKES NEURONS FIRE MORE READILY

Increased release of CRF causes neurons in the limbic system and amygdalae to fire much more readily than normal. This happens because CRF has the direct neurotransmitter effect in the brain of lowering the requisite threshold required for neurons to fire. This means that in the presence of more CRF *less* stimulation is needed to get a neuron to release its electrical charge towards another neuron. In fact, studies show that neurons are firing about two times more often than normal in the presence of excessive CRF.

TOO MUCH NEURAL FIRING CAUSES BRAIN AGITATION, SENSITISATION AND DISTRESS

Since CRF increases neural firing rates, it follows that when the amygdalae and HPA axis are subjected to larger amounts of CRF that there is an increase in the neural firing rates within the limbic system and sensory inputs, culminating in more frequent and intense signals of 'bottom-up' salience in the capacity to detect threat, fear and other disturbing phenomena.

This increase in signalling intensity makes the brain more *agitated* and *sensitised* to inputs (making them more salient and likely to break through into our conscious awareness) and leads directly to the mental *distress* we feel following stressful life events. In the presence of increased CRF we become hyper-alert to frightening, threatening, and disturbing mental phenomena, which may arise as any sort of mentation: including sensations, feelings, thoughts, images or memories following stressful life events.

HOW DOES THE INCREASE IN CRF OCCUR AT A CELLULAR LEVEL?

During periods of intense, ongoing stress like what is experienced during stressful life events, specific promoter proteins move into the cell nuclei of CRF-producing neurons (brain cells) and attach to defined promoter sites, switching on genes to code for the increased production of CRF. Many studies with mammals have been able to identify larger amounts of an immediate early gene-product called *c-fos* in CRF-producing brain cells following chronic stress.

Once these genes are switched on, they continue to produce larger amounts of specific CRF proteins while the threat is present. Once the threat has passed, then repressor proteins are activated to move into the cell nuclei and switch off CRF-producing genes, allowing the brain levels of CRF to return to normal.

The duration of this increased CRF output is likely to be dependent on the severity of the stress. In my work, I have found that once people *stop* paying attention to their distress the brain agitation due to increased CRF diminishes, and returns to normal over a period of about six months to two years, roughly in accordance with the severity of the stressful life event, with more severe ones taking longer. However, once people have stopped paying attention to their internal agitation, it no longer bothers them and they are effectively 'free' from its effects, *so long as they refrain from ever paying attention to it.*

On the other hand, where people *keep* paying attention by constant over-worrying and focus on their distress, the brain continues to perceive ongoing threat and repressor proteins remain inactivated, thereby keeping CRF-genes switched on and allowing the heightened brain agitation to continue unabated, perhaps for decades or even a lifetime. Where CRF is over-activated for years, it can result in people feeling excessively hyped-up and unpleasantly distressed for very long stretches of time.

HIGHER CRF-INDUCED BRAIN AGITATION LEADS TO PAYING MORE ATTENTION

Higher levels of CRF-induced brain agitation lead to more threat-related, frightening, disturbing and intense mentations. By 'mentations' I mean the conscious experience of mental events including sensations, feelings, thoughts, images or memories.

Since we are receiving more intense and frequent threat-warnings from our lower brain sensory inputs than usual, our higher (and conscious) brain regions, especially our attentional systems (ACC and DLPFC – please see Appendix) are much more inclined to pay attention to these disturbing phenomena in case we really are in danger.

MENTAL VERSUS EXTERNAL THREATS

If we really were in danger (for example, if our food or water supply was running out) this would not be a problem, because paying attention would benefit us and help us survive. For example, we would be prompted by increased CRF output to have intense mentations about how we could extend ourselves over the coming months to find more food or water. Then, once the threat was resolved we would no longer pay attention to it, allowing our CRF levels to gradually return to normal.

On the other hand, nowadays, our threats are mostly mental, like losing a job, failing an exam or receiving harsh, ongoing criticism. The events we face may be very unpleasant, but they are usually not life threatening. Yet our 'reptilian' brain still perceives the stressful life event as life-threatening and sets off a full CRF response that causes massive brain agitation and sensitisation despite the fact that we are usually not in any 'real' or serious danger.

All this uncontained neural firing from CRF then prompts our higher attentional brain systems to pay attention to the overly intense, threatening and catastrophic neural agitation. Of course, we can pay attention *endlessly* to mental phenomena, since there are effectively no limits to the number of sensations, feelings, thoughts, images or memories we can generate and focus upon. If we habituate or get used to one theme we can easily shift our attention onto another more threatening theme keeping the 'threat' ongoing.

When a threat is mental, not only can we speedily skip from one thought, image, feeling, sensation, or memory to another but, because *we do not have such clear signals* from the outside environment it is easy to pay attention to these phenomena and worry about them or focus on them for hours every day, leading us into ongoing cycles of distress.

In contrast, we tend to either die (of dehydration or hunger) or solve the problem when we have an external life-threatening event. Also, once the external threat has passed then we are constantly *cued* by our external environment (by flowing rivers or plentiful food) that the threat is over and we no longer need to mentally focus upon it.

PAYING ATTENTION INADVERTENTLY HOOKS US INTO OUR NORMAL LEARNING CYCLE

According to ST, it is precisely when we pay too much attention to these intense CRF-caused mentations that we make them escalate in number, frequency and intensity, thereby encouraging us to pay even more attention to them and thereby setting up self-reinforcing cycles of anxiety and distress.

This happens because as soon as we pay attention, we *inadvertently* tap into our **normal**, yet mightily powerful human ability to learn whatever is targeted in our focused attention.

Of course, our normal human learning processes have to be self-reinforcing so that we can acquire and build vast amounts of knowledge based on past learning, consolidation and recall. Yet we also have to be able to flexibly lose old, irrelevant knowledge that no longer serves us well so that it no longer interferes in our present calculations.

ST contends that *paying attention* is the perfect mechanism that directs our brains about exactly what to retain and what to discard. Paying attention allows us to *select* precise information. If we pay attention we avidly learn whatever material is targeted in our attentional focus, whereas if we fail to pay attention we rapidly degrade and break apart our synapses (more on this later) easily forgetting their content.

Unfortunately, paying attention to CRF-caused mentations readily draws us into our **normal** reinforced learning cycle and we unintentionally make our unwanted, distressing and disturbing themes and mentations a larger and larger presence in our brains keeping us cycling in anxiety and distress.

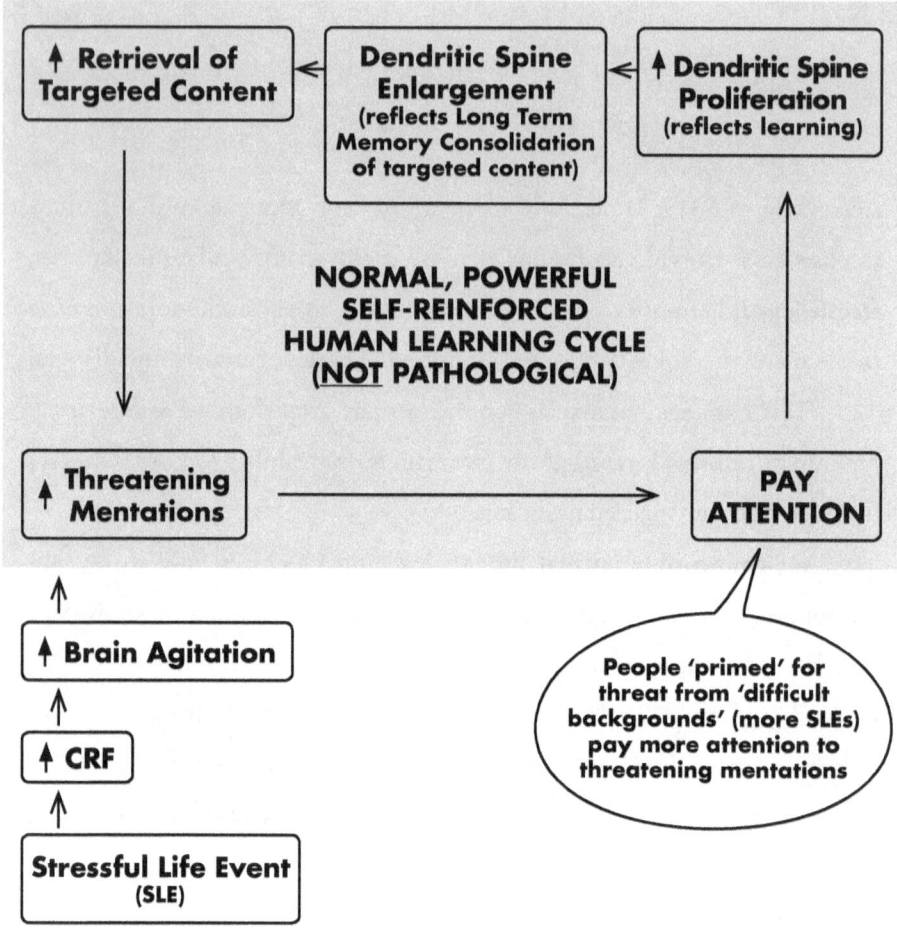

How we can 'learn' anxiety and other forms of psychological distress

These cycles of anxiety are often referred to as 'anxiety disorders' by health professionals, yet they are more likely just people paying attention to anxiety-related material and inadvertently learning it, thereby making it a larger and larger presence in their brains over time. Furthermore, it is probable that many other so-called 'mental disorders' such as depression, body image, psychosis, personality and impulse-control 'disorders' work the same way and may have also been incorrectly labelled.

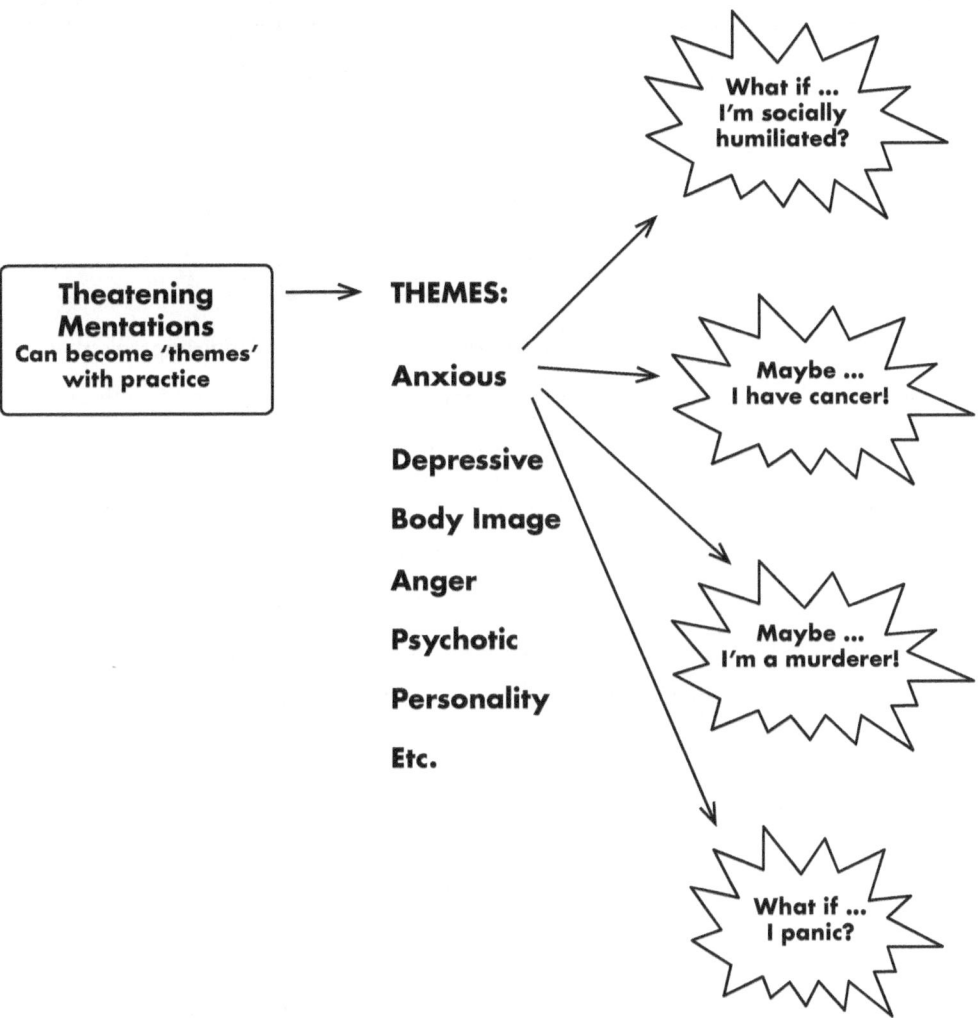

When we 'practice' paying attention, then over time we can develop a huge variety of 'themes' which have probably been wrongly identified as different mental 'disorders'

According to ST, there is nothing whatsoever pathological in the brains of anxious people, since our brains are doing exactly what they have evolved for – which is learning whatever material we bring into our focused attention. From the perspective of our brains, learning about anxiety is no different to learning about mathematics, music or geography and our brains will learn them all equally and super-efficiently just by paying attention.

WHAT HAPPENS IN OUR BRAINS WHEN WE PAY ATTENTION?

Although most cells in our brains are stable and do not change appreciably for their duration (this is why serious brain injury can be so catastrophic), neurons associated with learning and memory are highly flexible.

At a neurological level when we pay attention fascinating things happen. With better microscope techniques developed recently we have been able for the first time to observe single synapses and many important processes within them that relate directly to how we learn and remember. In fact, we seem to have found the actual *material basis* of learning and memory within our brains.

This material basis occurs within tiny but highly flexible protrusions called *dendritic spines* that *pop-up* or *retract* along particular dendrites ('branches' of brain cells), largely dependent upon whether or not we are paying attention. As soon as we pay attention, thin, spindly spines can be observed popping-up in disproportionate numbers along specific 'spiny' neurons that connect lower and higher brain regions and along other neurons related to learning and memory.

As soon as dendritic spines pop-up they release attractor chemicals to draw other neurons in the nearby vicinity in towards them, potentially creating *synapses* – which are simply connections between brain cells. Once synapses are formed, if we pay further attention we create more 'traffic' (in the form of electrical and chemical signals) across those synapses causing changes to the dendritic spines. Increased traffic makes the dendritic spines start to enlarge and change shape, becoming less like thin, spindly threads and more like stubby or solid mushrooms.

The larger, more stable shapes occur as the number of post-synaptic receptors increases (requiring a larger capsule) in connection with gene expression and protein synthesis which occur when we lay down long-term memory. In this way, the initial popping-up of thin, spindly dendritic spines can be seen as the material representation of *learning*, whereas the consolidation of the larger, more stable shapes with increased receptors can be seen as the material representation of further consolidation and *long-term memory* (*LTM*) formation.

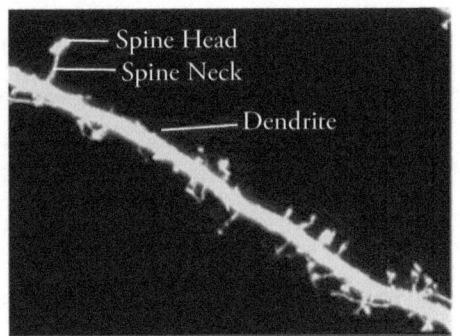 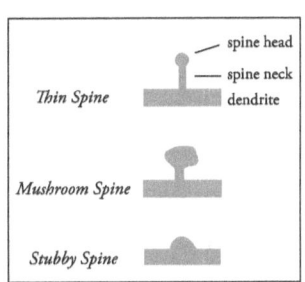

Dendritic spine shapes

When each dendritic spine pops-up initially, it has the genetic potential to be a fully-functioning synapse and it is compartmentalised off, so that messages do not 'leak' to surrounding spines. In this way, each spine can make its own specific contribution, perhaps representing part of a very simple image, sensation, thought or concept. Since we know that neurons that *fire together, wire together*, it is likely that close proximity of neurons and their dendritic spines leads to related (or associated) content within synapses.

Each dendritic spine can input one vote if it has traffic (signals) crossing it but if there is no traffic it will not vote and therefore not influence the parent neuron to fire. The parent neuron itself only fires on an *all or none* basis.

If a requisite threshold is reached by the number of inputted votes from many dendritic spines (and this can be helped by increased CRF), then a neuron will fire and thereby increase the probability of down-stream firing of other neurons.

OUR AMAZING FRONTAL AND PREFRONTAL BRAIN

No doubt you have heard of the amazing capacities of our frontal cortex and in particular our prefrontal cortex which is the most forward part of our brains directly behind our forehead. In humans, our frontal brain has grown exponentially compared with all other animals and it is largely responsible for many of the things that make us human.

It allows us to pay focussed attention, think rationally, to plan, to understand past, present and future, to grasp abstraction, to be flexible, spontaneous and imaginative, and, it is where *consciousness* is experienced. Very importantly, our prefrontal cortex allows us to pay attention to important brain signals and influence them by amplifying or diminishing them and essentially acting as 'the boss' of the whole brain.

Within our prefrontal cortex, our attentional system can voluntarily regulate the intensity or salience of signals in distant neurons. For example, once it receives signals from distant areas it can *voluntarily* signal back and adjust the firing rate of those distant neurons, exerting top-down influence by reducing signals or nudging neural populations towards synchronous firing. This provides humans with conscious control over our brains, very different from all other animals. It makes nonsense of poor scientific comparisons between humans and other animals, such as those that argue that some types of chimpanzees' rape and therefore human rape is somehow justified. Unlike all other animals, humans *always* have the capacity for control provided by our exceptional prefrontal cortex which might be thought of as the material representation of 'Free Will'.

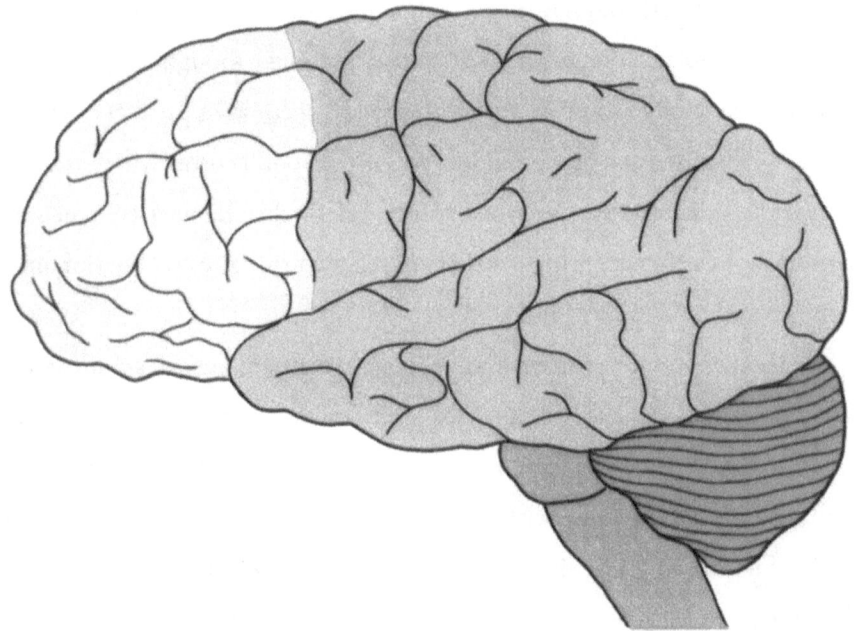

The enormous human prefrontal cortex (light area)

SYNCHRONOUS FIRING

Studies show that synchronous firing in the brain represents *paying focused attention* and leads to massive amplification and activation of downstream neural networks. Synchronous firing also results in disproportionate dendritic spine proliferation (popping up), synaptic strengthening and spine-head enlargement indicative of long-term memory consolidation in activated downstream networks. These downstream networks may be closely or more vaguely connected in synapse content to the initially activated neural population – allowing lateral and more or less relevant concepts to be retrieved into the mix of 'possible' mentations at any one time.

The more downstream networks are recruited, the more likely their signals will break through from our sub-threshold or pre-conscious domain into our conscious domain as sensations, feelings, thoughts, images or memories that we become aware of. Awareness then often prompts further voluntary examination and attention by our prefrontal cortex which readily results in additional synchronous firing and further downstream neural activation – easily becoming a self-reinforcing learning, consolidation and retrieval cycle.

These normal learning and memory processes reveal an amazing and invaluable capacity for humans to learn targeted material. On the other hand, repeated attention towards unwanted mental themes will inadvertently lock people with equal efficiency into this highly effective and self-reinforcing learning machine. Our brains will learn *whatever* we direct them to learn: constructive or destructive. Fortunately, at the helm of this powerful learning process is our ability (within our prefrontal cortex) to *voluntarily* choose the target of our attention.

ST ADVOCATES USING OUR AMAZING LEARNING CYCLE TO OUR ADVANTAGE

What is truly amazing about dendritic spines is that they are so responsive that they may pop-up and then retract and disappear after only a few seconds (if there is no follow-up reinforcement by paying further attention), or they might pop-up and remain for a few moments, a few days, a few weeks, a few months or a few years, or they might pop-up and last for a lifetime. The cognitive areas of our brains are that flexible!

What determines how long spines pop-up for is how much attention we continue to pay to those specific synapses and, the good news is that what we pay attention to is 100% **voluntary**! For example, if we decide not to pay attention, then we will reduce the traffic crossing our synapses and we weaken them. Stopping paying attention not only weakens specific inputs, but we can stop them from 'voting' and thereby reduce the downstream amplification of whole networks and the synchronous firing created by paying attention. Over time, without attention, the synapses weaken and degrade to such an extent that they break apart and the dendritic spine retracts back into the parent dendrite, disappearing along with its input capacity.

We humans are super-efficient, what we don't use we lose! Literally. Think about how easy it is to lose muscle if you stop exercising. Without constant reinforcement of its necessity, muscle starts falling away in no time at all. Humans are lean machines and for maximum efficiency we will not carry anything that is not necessary. Our brains are no different. Anything that is not regularly paid attention to fades. Our recall gets increasingly vague until we really struggle to recall much of the detail at all.

What I am suggesting in ST is that we can choose to use these biological processes to our advantage to deal with unwanted mental material. In the past, you may have thought you *had* to pay attention to these anxious, disturbing, frightening, annoying, self-sabotaging mentations, but **really you don't**. You may have also believed that once you paid attention to these disturbing and threatening mentations they were so frightening that you then had to endlessly search for solutions, even if they were ineffective or self-sabotaging to try to keep safe. There is more on this in the next chapter, but trust me, **you don't**!

These anxious mentations have just become a well-reinforced neural habit – where we just pay them attention because they feel *salient* from too much CRF-induced brain agitation and we then keep learning, consolidating and retrieving them out of habit. For example, a dreaded thought might be triggered, we pay attention to it and we instigate the whole process of dendritic spine proliferation and consolidation, leading us to pay further attention whereby we inadvertently activate related networks and dredge-up similar or lateral content to add to the mix and really frighten ourselves! Being so distressed encourages us to pay yet more attention, and so the cycle exacerbates.

But the reality is that we can decide at any moment to *stop learning* the unwanted material. This is no different to deciding that we have had enough of physics and we are going to stop learning it in future. Very soon we will have fewer and fewer physics thoughts until, over time and with enough neglect, we struggle to recall even the basic principles.

Once you understand the neural processes, you can exploit them to serve you better. Once you fully grasp that within ST there is **no pathology** happening here and it is all just part of the **normal** learning process, then you can simply decide to stop learning any unwanted material. Your brain will completely cooperate with you since this is just the usual way it learns, remembers or forgets. In short, you can make the firm decision to give up paying attention to the things you want to mentally lose, and start paying attention instead to a constructive life!

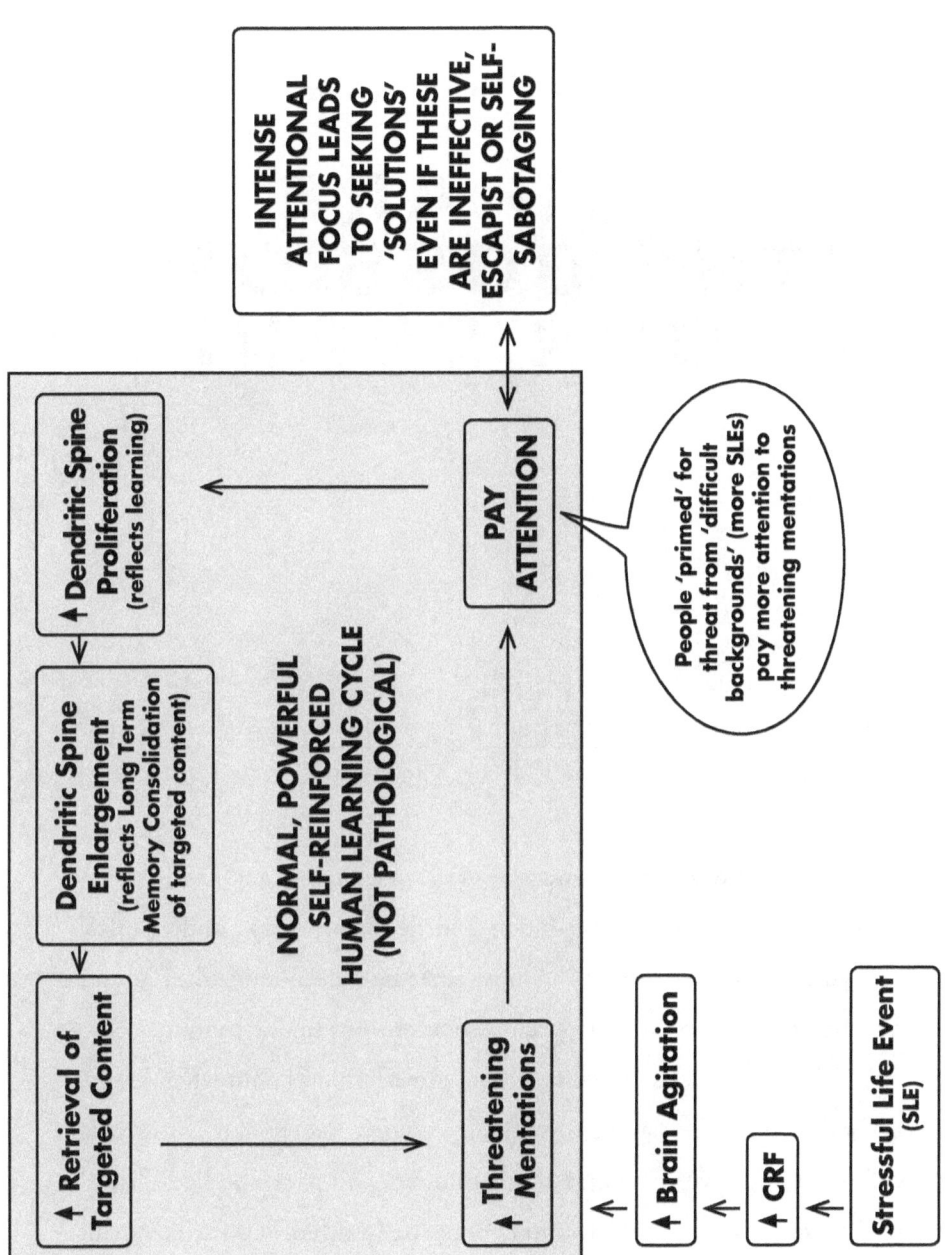

We don't have to pay attention to threatening mentations and 'learn' them and neither do we need to seek desperate 'solutions' to the dreaded threat that may be self-sabotaging, ineffective or escapist

WHAT HAPPENS IN OUR BRAINS? | 39

CHAPTER THREE

YOU ARE THE BOSS OF YOUR BRAIN

TAKING RESPONSIBILITY – THE SIMPLE, BUT CRUCIAL MENTAL SHIFT REQUIRED IN SMART THERAPY

You may have already guessed, but one of the most important reasons to have read Chapter Two was because understanding the neurology underlying ST helps you realise that even at the most basic biological level adult humans have the brain-power to control the mentations our brains contain.

What this means in reality, is that our decisions about what material our brains learn, by paying attention, *really do* matter and will provide positive or negative outcomes that profoundly impact our lives. This is not dissimilar to making a decision about the health of our cardiovascular system when we decide whether or not to be fit. We can choose to exercise and eat well or we can choose to lie around eating chocolate and potato chips and becoming increasingly unfit.

In short, working within the ST approach means understanding that the buck stops with you! It is your **choice** what material you decide to lay down in your brain and it is **your** choice what material you decide not to lay down. The choices you make will have clear consequences for the rest of your life and for your happiness.

Of course this was not the case when we were children. As children none of us were responsible for the content of our brains since our brains were not fully developed and therefore unable to exercise full adult frontal and attentional control. Also, as children, we had no choice about what environment we were born into so we all learnt whatever our good, bad, mixed or indifferent environment offered up to us without discrimination.

Many brain habits that are both use*ful* and use*less* are set up in childhood, but what the ST neurology allows us to understand is that we have the brain-power as adults to decide to change any unwanted brain habits if we wish. Also, ST neurology helps us to realise that although anxious and distressing thoughts, feelings, sensations, images and memories are initially generated by too much CRF following stressful life events, it is **we** who have the power to reinforce or not reinforce those mentations by the degree of attention we pay them.

It was likely never your fault (especially in childhood) that you experienced stressful life events, and it was certainly never your fault that your brain pumped out too much CRF giving you frightening, distressing and disturbing thoughts or feelings – but once you know as an adult that you have the power to either limit or extend those effects, **then it makes complete sense to take charge**!

Even though you may not have realised it before, you now know you have 100% control over what you decide to pay attention to – your prefrontal cortex is *that* good! Once and for all you are able to get into the driver's seat of your own life and project your own values onto the life **you** choose to live instead of living out the old, useless, self-sabotaging habits someone else directed you to learn when you were a child.

It is so liberating (and a little scary) to realise that you are entirely responsible for the content of your own brain going forward. Suddenly, when you properly realise this you become grown-up overnight. Essentially, it is **your** brain and you are responsible for what you put into it. No need to blame others any longer: the content is up to **you**. No-one has a gun to your head now you are grown up!

If you have been holding onto the child or victim role, you must now relinquish it! As painful as it is to step up and take full responsibility from now on you must do it in order to move forward. Basically, you have one life and even though many terrible things may have happened in the past that you were **not** responsible for, you now have the power to shape your own brain however you want!

Now you know that you have the brain control and it is entirely your choice what you decide to pay attention to, be aware that whatever you choose to pay attention to will come to literally *fill your brain*.

It is no good saying things like 'I just woke up feeling lousy – then my day just went downhill from there'. Even though I know it is upsetting to wake up feeling lousy and I wish that you did not feel that way, it is important that you understand that we *all* have had plenty of days where we wake up feeling lousy but it is our choice whether we pay any further attention to those unwanted feelings.

Moreover, it is our choice whether we *add* more words and thoughts to that 'lousy' biochemical feeling making it a bigger presence in our brain. It is our choice whether we pay *so much* attention to that 'lousy' feeling that we consolidate it into long term memory enabling it to be retrieved over and over in the future, making us anticipate more and more 'lousy' days from then on. More 'lousy' days means less happiness and less satisfaction and pleasure in our lives. It also means we spend our lives contemplating our lousiness instead of doing the things that enable us to live constructive and meaningful lives. We can be so focused on our own misery that we fail to make important contributions to wider society.

Until we **decide** to stop paying attention and stop reinforcing this unwanted 'lousy' feeling, it will keep on being a large presence in our brains. Yet, it doesn't have to be this way; we can quite easily decide to pay attention to alternative material. By way of alternative, we could choose to totally ignore the 'lousy' feeling and just get up and go on with some constructive activities, irrespective of how 'lousy' we feel. For example, we could get up, have a shower, make a healthy breakfast and read the newspaper. In short, we can just decide to stop paying attention to our 'lousy' feelings. These are all choices that each of us has the power to make just by the sheer luck of having a human brain with such a powerful frontal lobe.

Grasping that you are in charge of your brain from now on – that you and *only* you are responsible for the content of your brain – is the simple mental shift that **has** to be made in order for you to overcome your difficulties. **Nothing** will change until you fully grasp this point. Maybe you need to say it out aloud: ***I am now totally responsible for the content of my own brain!***

In other words, what you choose to learn by paying attention will then have real and concrete consequences for your life. You might like your brain to contain lots of skills and interests and you might like your brain to contain lots of creativity, friendliness, warmth, sociability, love and music, and you might like your brain to be articulate and assertive. Most likely, you will **not** want your brain to contain lots of anxious, frightening, threatening, disturbing, angry, addictive, guilty or suicidal mentations.

Up until this point you may have thought these distressing mentations *just took you over*. That you had no part to play in their presence – they had perhaps *always* seemed to be there – like they were just part of who you were. I certainly believed this in my earlier life when I was in the depths of despair.

But let me be absolutely clear about this: It is **only** you paying attention to them that keeps them going. If you stop paying them attention they gradually become fewer and fewer until they are effectively gone. I bet in many cases paying attention has become so much of a habit that you have not even been aware that you are doing it.

I bet it has become such a habit that you have had no idea how instrumental you have been in driving the whole process. While the difficulties would have initially started with a stressful life event and too much CRF output, **it is you and *only* you, who is now keeping the problem going!**

Every day that you are spending hours worrying, ruminating, focusing on unwanted habits you are strengthening them in your brain and making them come back at you ten-fold. As unbelievable as it may sound, it is **you** who is keeping your misery going!

Please understand that from a ST perspective, **there is nothing wrong with you or your brain!** Assuming you are not severely brain damaged, then your brain is roughly as good as any other brain – otherwise you would not be reading or comprehending this book. The problem is simply **what** you have been choosing to pay attention to and for how long.

Now I know I am labouring the point here, but if you don't thoroughly get this point then you will not be able to progress in ST. You will continue to think things *happen* ***to*** *you*, that you are a *victim* of circumstance, that you have no power over your own brain. You will continue to think that your brain is somehow dysfunctional or pathological and that it requires medication and the whole mental health system to intervene and fix it. Trust me, your brain is doing ***exactly*** what it has evolved to do, it is learning whatever you are paying attention to.

However, since there is no such thing in life as decisions without negative consequences, and it is only in fairy tales that any decision is all good or all bad, I must explain the costs to you of your decision to assume you are in charge of your own brain. There are two main costs of this choice. First, you have to be willing to accept the responsibility that you are no longer a victim and, if in future you slide back to your old habits and are not happy, then it is you who is responsible and no-one else. It is you who is somehow failing yourself and it is your job to re-gather your resources and put a quick end to any lapses where you have accidentally gone back to paying attention to disturbing mentations.

Obviously there are exceptions to the notion that you are completely responsible, such as when truly uncontrollable and horrific environmental stressors occur like war, torture, extreme poverty, disease and starvation. Interestingly though, as I have seen from my work, even in these extreme scenarios people can exercise some control and bear these harsh circumstances relatively well or they can relinquish all power and bear them badly.

Second, you have to be willing to embrace new and constructive ways of behaving. This involves not allowing yourself to lose control and go back to old, useless, self-sabotaging anxiety behaviours. Even though it is true that most of the new behaviours you will be doing will be much more inspiring, interesting and fun, remember that your brain has been in the habit of doing the old, useless behaviours for a long time and, old habits often feel familiar and comfortable even if they are self-sabotaging.

At times you will have to decide to do what is tougher, *not* what is easier. You will have to commit to being strong when you might prefer to hide and curl up in a ball like a victim. You can decide to call yourself to account – being honest with yourself when you are giving yourself an easy way out. In short, you need to decide that **you are worth saving**! To do this you have to work for your *future* self not give in to your *old, self-sabotaging* self by repeating useless habits just because they feel more familiar or comfortable.

Mostly though, you can feel over-joyed since the positive consequences are enormous and easily outweigh relinquishing the victim role. You can **enjoy** learning to be mentally tough. It feels great to be **free**! Free from your difficult past. Free from the old, frustrating habits that kept you down and kept you miserable. According to ST, you can be freed from your anxiety forever if you just take responsibility and understand that by paying attention to your anxiety it is you, and only you, who is keeping it going! Be clear: You can decide to stop paying that attention, at any time you like!

A great thing about learning to take responsibility is that it teaches you over time that you have **agency**, **skills**, **ambition** and **power**. By realising the buck stops with you, it makes you step up and take charge of your own brain content with agency and initiative, developing a myriad of skills that enable you to reach for your dreams and ambitions, which then gives you more and more power and strength over time.

This will be a virtuous cycle, rather than a vicious cycle of anxiety, despair, passivity and withdrawal in life. You will be able to be truly happy and truly productive in life. But you must fully understand that it is up to you! No-one but you can save yourself!

Initially, this is tricky to fully understand, as many people who are reading this book will have come from difficult backgrounds. Difficult backgrounds often teach people to be passive, anxious and withdrawing preventing them from learning to come forward and properly engage in the world.

These backgrounds can ensure children learn the despair and hopelessness that comes with knowing there is nothing they can do to save themselves: no action they can take lest they be punished. So many people in our society have learnt they are victims (because in childhood they were) but unbeknown to themselves they have unnecessarily kept practicing victimhood as adults without even knowing it, unaware that their own frontal brain could save them.

I was the worst offender. Even though I acted tough on the outside, blaming others, smoking, drinking, and often getting angry for no good reason, underneath I felt scared, anxious, powerless, and out of control. I was passive about my ability to change, yet at the same time I was terrified for what I could see was going to be a *very* messed up future if I did not change.

For years, I tried desperately to recruit others to help me in the hope they would find answers and show me the way forward. I would choose very skilled boyfriends and friends in the hope they would pull me through life using their skills and know-how because I did not have my own. The trouble was that while I was busy looking to others to help me, I was being passive and failing to take charge myself. Every time other people solved my problems, I was teaching myself that I was incapable of standing on my own two feet.

Then came my lowest point where I was so far down in the hole of despair that I felt I could go no lower without actually dying. At that point, I remember realising the hole was so black and so deep that no one could reach me. I was utterly alone in my frozen, desolate world. No one could reach me or help me. None of my skilled boyfriends, friends or acquaintances could rescue me.

I had to help myself – no one could save me but me! It hit me like a thunderbolt! **I had to save myself!** That crucial realisation made me dig deep into myself. Every part of my life force dug in at that moment and committed to me saving myself. In that moment I had thrown off much of my 'victimhood' and finally stepped up to take responsibility for my own life. Without that awareness, nothing would have changed.

I decided on one immediate improvement. I was determined to find a way to get into university to improve myself, because I figured that at least that would keep me learning and perhaps knowledge would help me find a solution to my predicament. Getting into University though was no easy task, as I had an appalling academic record punctuated with school absences. Nonetheless, I chased that goal single-mindedly and eventually found a way in.

Once at university I became responsible for passing or failing – again, there was no one to rescue me. It was sink or swim. Even though I was struggling with the very basics of academia since I had missed much of my early schooling, I was also highly aware of how bleak life could be with never-ending dead-end jobs. This made me determined to pass and if that meant taking proper responsibility, then so be it.

Taking more responsibility meant that I reflected on myself more and, over time brought me to the realisation that I was somehow keeping many of my problems going – since there was a repetitiveness and a compulsion to many of my dysfunctional patterns. Although the stressful life events of my childhood would have started my distress, there was also something I was doing that was keeping them alive.

For example, every time I put a cigarette or alcoholic drink in my mouth it 'felt' to me like a defiant, tough, 'stuff you' rebellion against my mother – it sort of made me feel good about myself, as though with every drink or every cigarette I was confirming my power and strength in opposing her. I felt bold and brave, and these self-harming habits felt like nourishment.

Yet, at the same time I was aware that these substances were destroying me. They held no real nourishment. Every cigarette was another step closer to emphysema or lung cancer or every alcoholic drink was another step closer to addiction, liver failure or dementia.

I was also aware that in my adulthood there was no longer anyone physically around me that I needed to defy, resist or defend against. By now I was bigger and stronger than my mother and other people were almost always kind to me. Bit by bit, I started to open up to the idea that, as an adult, the only person who was keeping me doing these self-depreciating and self-sabotaging behaviours was **myself**.

Although at that stage I did not know exactly *how* I was doing it, it was absolutely essential to my recovery to realise I was somehow driving the process of my own misery. This allowed me to take the necessary responsibility and enquire about how I might be doing this.

Once I started asking more questions of myself, I began to realise that my childhood fear of my mother had locked me into a hard, stubborn, closed-minded resistance. I came to understand that there was a price to pay for creating an impenetrable protective shield against my mother, with cigarettes and alcohol that numbed my feelings and made me feel 'tougher'.

The price was an unintended consequence, whereby in closing out my mother I inadvertently also closed down my own access to my softer and more vulnerable self. Without access and the regular practice of mentally visiting my softer self, it had started to die.

Recall that with our highly flexible brain, if you don't use it, you lose it. Without regular visitations to my soft heart, I was becoming increasingly hard, impenetrable and closed down. This was a far cry from the bold and brave person I had previously thought myself.

In working my way through this problem, it occurred to me, that the *way* I had done this was largely by the story I told myself. I realised that my 'tough', 'defiant', rebellious and 'stuff you' response to the fear I felt towards my mother as a child and teenager was, when really placed under the microscope, actually a 'hard' 'closed-minded' and 'invulnerable' response.

Notice the subtlety: Tough, defiant, rebellious and a 'stuff you' attitude are more appealing attributes since they imply inner strength and an independent sense of self. On the other hand, being hard, closed-minded, or invulnerable are unappealing attributes and no one wants to think of themselves in these ways. I especially hated to think of myself this way.

Notice the subtle lie, the subtle sleight-of-hand that allowed me to keep telling myself a lie that kept me smoking and drinking for years since it supported what I liked to think of as my rather 'bold' 'brave' and 'defiant' sense of self. Once I got real with myself and understood that it was actually a strategy in closing down, becoming hard and impenetrable, then I quickly started working out how to quit these self-sabotaging habits.

Even though it was a big shock to have to throw off my victim shackles and realise I was responsible for my *ongoing* misery, it also helped me enormously to move forward in my life. Gradually I came to understand that if I acknowledged and took responsibility for my contribution to my ongoing misery, then that also meant that there was something I could actually do about it.

On the other hand, I knew that if I remained a total victim with zero contribution and took zero responsibility for my actions then by simple rules of logic, there was absolutely zero I could do to improve matters. Even though, it is easy to think that taking responsibility would be a bitter pill to swallow (and one I resisted for many years), I can assure you that when

I finally took responsibility it felt fantastic! I finally had some answers that allowed me to get out of being 'stuck' in my life.

Something that I had pointedly avoided for most of my life, actually gave me **real power**! Suddenly I realised that if I was contributing then I could change that contribution and that meant I could somehow fix up my messed-up life, piece by piece. My mission then became one of *solving my contribution*, as opposed to drinking and smoking myself passively into oblivion as a powerless victim.

As I gradually grasped more and more biological, psychological and neurological knowledge at university and later in clinical practice it further empowered me at every stage, and I fully grasped that I was now completely responsible for the life I would live and for what my brain contained. I not only learned that I could stop being a victim, I learned that I **had** to stop being a victim and take charge *if* I wanted to improve.

With some careful thinking, we can all learn to step up and take charge. Be clear that the cavalry is not coming to rescue any of us. We are effectively alone in this world. We have to take responsibility as soon as possible for our lives or they quickly pass us by without us ever getting over our self-sabotaging, boring, useless and repetitive habits that are, in reality, long outdated, having arisen mostly in our childhood and teenage years.

Believe me that failing to take responsibility can drag on for decades. I have seen many people in their sixties, seventies and beyond still resisting being responsible for their own lives. In the end, no one but you can make the decision about exactly what you want to learn and exactly what you would like to get rid of in your own brain. There is no time to waste; the power is completely in your hands to stop paying attention to all anxiety mentations, **if** you are willing to use it!

THE IMPORTANCE OF *ALWAYS* STAYING IN CONTROL

Another crucially important aspect of grasping the ST neurology from Chapter Two is that it allows us to realise that we can pretty much always stay fully in control over our own brains and therefore over our own bodies and our actions (behaviours).

SELF-SABOTAGING BEHAVIOURS

Paying attention to CRF-driven threat quite sensibly leads to an urge to find 'solutions'. However, until we grasp that it is our own attentional focus that *causes* the continuance of our threatening mentations, we can easily persist, and since there is no improvement, pay more and more attention to endlessly seeking other incorrect 'solutions'.

This directs our brain to build ever more synapses devoted to both our threat themes and our incorrect 'solutions' – making them, over time a larger and larger part of our brain and hence, our subjective experience.

These 'solutions', out of desperation, can often be self-sabotaging, escapist or have no actual effect upon the dreaded threat. For example, avoiding the number 7 or the colour black in case it causes a loved one to die.

Other 'solutions' can easily restrict our lives from normality, like refusing to drive in case we 'collapse at the wheel'. Refusing to drive means we never allow ourselves to take normal, everyday risks that would otherwise demonstrate that we are highly unlikely to 'collapse at the wheel'. Without this normal demonstration we continue to pay vigilant attention to the dreaded event and our 'solution' of avoidance thereby strengthens the *incorrect* belief that we would 'collapse at the wheel' if we did not avoid driving.

This same error can apply equally to avoidance of supermarkets, flying, lifts, germs, public transport or social exposure. It also applies with checking and other ineffectual 'solutions' where we inadvertently reinforce at a neural level the incorrect belief that it is our checking or ineffectual solution that prevents the dreaded event from occurring. For example, repetitively tapping three times so that that the plane does not crash.

Still other 'solutions' like alcohol, smoking, medications or drugs can have their own problems such as ongoing and dangerous addiction cycles. As you might expect, these self-sabotaging behaviours can increasingly encroach and can ultimately destroy our lives by taking up more and more of our time and mental space.

Once we utilise these self-sabotaging escape behaviours we can easily start to focus on the idea that we 'cannot cope' without employing them. For example, many people believe (completely wrongly) that they cannot cope with going to a social occasion without drinking alcohol, or they cannot cope with going out to dinner without over-eating, or they cannot cope with conflict without becoming aggressive or compliant, or they cannot cope with going in lifts and therefore must take the stairs or avoid the building altogether.

Once we engage with this idea that we 'cannot cope without escape' then we continue to pay attention to this incorrect idea and it and our other ineffectual 'solutions' get drawn into our normal learning cycle and reinforced alongside our other threatening mentations. Over time, with lots of attentional focus and reinforcement people can falsely come to believe that they 'must' escape no matter how much their escape behaviours are seriously harming them.

> **INTENSE ATTENTIONAL FOCUS LEADS TO SEEKING 'SOLUTIONS' EVEN IF THESE ARE INEFFECTIVE, ESCAPIST OR SELF-SABOTAGING**
>
> Paying attention to threat leads to an urge to find solutions. Even if, out of desperation, these 'solutions' are self-sabotaging, escapist or have no actual effect upon the dreaded threat. For example, avoiding the number 7 or the colour black in case it causes a loved one to die.
>
> *Until we realise it is our own attentional focus that causes the continuance of our threatening mentations,* we can easily persist (since our 'solutions' often don't work) and pay more and more attention to endlessly seeking more and more of these incorrect or misguided 'solutions'.
>
> This directs our brain to build ever more synapses devoted to both our threat themes and our 'solutions' – making them, over time a larger and larger part of our brain and hence, our subjective experience.
>
> Other 'solutions' like alcohol, smoking, medications or drugs can have their own problems such as addiction cycles or reinforcement of the belief that we are 'unable to cope' without them – thus keeping them going.
>
> Still other 'solutions' can easily lead to illogical brain connections and restrict our lives from normality, like refusing to drive in case we 'collapse at the wheel'. Refusing to drive means we never allow ourselves to take normal risks that would otherwise demonstrate that we are highly unlikely to 'collapse at the wheel'. Therefore, we continue to pay vigilant attention to the dreaded threat (collapse) and our 'solution' (not driving) thereby strengthening the *incorrect and illogical* brain connection that we would 'collapse at the wheel' if we did not avoid driving.
>
> As we persist with applying these misguided, ineffective, escapist and often self-sabotaging 'solutions' they can increasingly encroach and ultimately destroy our lives.

Paying attention to CRF-driven threat leads us to seek 'solutions' even if these 'solutions', out of desperation, are escapist, self-sabotaging or have no actual effect

In ST, not only do we need to fully take responsibility that the buck stops with us at an abstract level, but we need to grasp that the buck stops with us in terms of our behaviours every minute of every day. We **choose** our behaviours and we can **choose** to change them. The means to achieving control over our behaviours lies within our brains – and there will be no surprises that again, it is the frontal part of our brains that we predominantly utilise. In short, think of it like this: Your conscious, prefrontal cortex is **you**, and **you** are the *boss* of your brain!

As I have mentioned, besides determining what we pay attention to, our prefrontal cortex can speed (or hype) things up or it can slow things down neurologically in other parts of our brains by sending signals to distant neurons influencing their firing rates and encouraging them or not towards synchrony, and through this process our prefrontal cortex has the capacity to disregard our emotive limbic system if we so choose.

This is the essential biological liberation of humans over all other species – our prefrontal cortex has this executive control over other parts of our brains. It has the capacity to be functionally separate, objective, reflective, creative and self-organising, ensuring it is no slave to *biological determinism*. Our frontal brain and particularly our prefrontal cortex can be thought of as the material representation of free will, mental flexibility and ultimate self-control.

Yet the cost of such high levels of brain flexibility is that if we are not sufficiently aware and diligent, our emotions and limbic brain systems can be allowed to dominate. In fact, if I had to identify the central problem of *every* single person I have ever seen in my ST centre, it is that *everyone* is constantly giving themselves permission to *lose control*.

Losing control can occur by allowing anxiety or depressive rumination to prevail, losing control of anger, losing control of alcohol, drug or cigarette consumption, losing control of eating, losing control over violence, or losing control over psychotic thoughts. A huge amount of human misery arises from letting ourselves lose control.

So obviously, despite having a brain that gives us extraordinary levels of mental control many people still fail to realise they have this ultimate control.

This is not surprising because we only have one brain, and if we encounter distress as children and our difficult environment literally trains our brains to pay attention to that distress (giving our limbic system more dominance) then we easily continue into adulthood **never realising** we can exercise much higher levels of brain control if we recruit more of our frontal brain into our daily lives.

Again, I was the worst offender. For many years I genuinely believed that I could not control my thoughts or other mentations – they seemed to just take me over as if against my will. Equally, many of my behaviours felt involuntary. When I had an urge to smoke cigarettes I felt *compelled* to act on it. When I had an urge to over-eat, I felt *compelled* to act on it. Similarly, when I became angry I felt *compelled* to act on it.

I remember describing to my husband (then boyfriend) the *physical* sensation and rush of rage as it shot upwards like a powerful bolt of lightning through my body exploding outwards through my actions of yelling or screaming or striking out in what I believed was self-defence. I *truly* thought I was a victim and that I had no control when it came to my anger.

But that was the victim speaking: the victim turned perpetrator and bully. Indeed, I realised later that it was the victim story of having 'no control' that enabled me to justify and rationalise indefensible, angry behaviour. If I could not control it, then I was not responsible I told myself (or more to the point, *lied* to myself).

Moreover, deep in my victim-world I saw others as all-powerful compared with me. Given I believed I had no control in this 'unfair' world it seemed only reasonable to play dirty and outside the rules of fairness and kindness whenever necessary. Within this 'no-holds-barred' victim-domain it became justifiable to rip off the gloves, scream, throw things and have tantrums.

Once after a particularly bad fit of rage in my 20's, my (now) husband very calmly and quietly said to me that even though he was madly in love with me that he would leave me if I ever lost control of my anger again.

That shocked me. Not because he was threatening to leave (who wouldn't!) but because someone was quietly and calmly telling me that I had the power and control to *not* act in accordance with my 'out-of-control' feelings. As strange as it sounds, that thought had never before occurred to me!

Suddenly I knew he was absolutely right. All those years I had believed I had no control (that my anger would just *take me over*) and in the blink of an eye I realised actually, I had 100% control. It didn't really matter what I felt, I did not have to act on it. I could **always** stay in control!

In fact, if I wanted to keep my relationship it was imperative that I *not* act on my feelings of anger no matter how intense they felt. Anyway, when I properly thought about it I realised that most of my angry and intense feelings were, in any case, just loaded up ammunition and explosives from old and outdated wars from my childhood and adolescence. All the pent-up anger had very little relevance in the present day.

In deciding to take control, I further threw off the victim yoke. I had to get real with myself about my past behaviours and ask myself questions about the consequences of my largely unrestrained anger.

Within seconds of being told I would be left alone if I did not stop my anger, I knew that I had turned from a childhood victim into an adult bully. I had become a version of my brutal mother, albeit never towards children, but certainly towards adults who scared me. For nearly all of my life, I had loathed my mother for her cruelty, yet (like so many victims) I had become a bully myself **without even noticing it**!

Amazingly, I had been protected from this vital self-knowledge by my powerless 'victim' role. In our society, victims are usually thought of as helpless and meek, but when I became honest with myself, I knew from first-hand experience just how ferocious victims could easily become.

As soon as I owned up to having become a bully, I felt deeply embarrassed and ashamed. How could this have happened? At least though, in facing it squarely, I knew I was **never, ever** going to be a bully again! I was determined that it would only happen over my dead body!

What was truly amazing though, was that from that moment of me deciding to have zero tolerance for my expressions of anger and bullying, the physical anger bolt that used to rise up inside me virtually disappeared overnight!

This was quite unbelievable, because rage and anger were extremely well-cemented and well-practiced neurological strategies for me at that time. Yet, once I knew for certain that I was *never* going to act on these feelings again, the anger bolt barely bothered to appear!

When it *very rarely* made its presence felt it was so much weaker (more like a little jolt), and it took very little effort to resist. Quickly over time, even the 'little jolt' petered out almost entirely and, after about two years, it was virtually undetectable, and just some vague, distant memory.

All of this was an important lesson for me about our human capacity to maintain frontal brain control and the lies we can easily tell ourselves to justify unjustifiable behaviour. In the end, it only took one clear decision over 30 years ago which meant I have never lost or wanted to lose my temper again.

Yet, when you analyse it, all that really happened was that I became motivated (by realising I had become a bully) to recruit the excellent control of my frontal brain over my well-practiced but out-of-control limbic system. This is a capacity all humans share, just because we are lucky enough to be born human!

PART TWO:

WHAT IS THE METHOD OF SMART THERAPY?

CHAPTER FOUR

STEP ONE: KEEP YOUR BEHAVIOURS USEFUL, EFFECTIVE AND NEVER SELF-SABOTAGING

PREAMBLE

It is important that you get the specific information about context and how to apply the steps from the following chapters before you launch into ST. So, read the book until the end and then (if you need to) come back to these chapters and follow the method.

The ST method is very simple and easy to use and is based on two decades of investigation and trial and error with thousands of people. There are essentially four steps which are easily remembered and which ought to be applied in challenging situations.

Although I will present the four steps to you in numerical order, they are actually all meant to be combined into a very quickly-done package, where their order might change slightly and they are applied (only taking a matter of seconds) more or less at the same time once you have worked out the detail involved in each step. Since they are so easy to remember and apply, my advice is to use them always, all the time and every day.

Also, even though these steps will help you to get you over anxiety, they are also useful *generally* in life and they can be applied to virtually any situation. Even though it is not the focus of this book, I have found in my centre that the ST method works for all sorts of problems including addiction, anger, depression, under or over eating and it even appears to vastly improve psychosis. Anyway, the point is that once any anxiety habits are cleared up, you can still use and apply these four steps in your life generally to help you stay on track and live a constructive life forever!

WHERE AM I COMING FROM?

There is one important point that I want to make before I go on any further, and that is that I am **not** coming from a moral/blame/judgmental perspective **ever** in this book. My comments come from what is called a 'teleological' paradigm, which focusses on outcome; rather than a 'deontological' paradigm, which focusses on right or wrong. So especially over the next few chapters where I am talking about behavioural change please do not accuse me of 'blaming the victim' because I am not, and would not.

On the other hand, although I never blame victims, this does not mean that I am always persuaded that victims behave in their own best interests. For example, even though a smoker may have initially been a 'victim' because she/he was targeted by cigarette companies as a vulnerable teenager and so became addicted to nicotine, I would *not* advocate that the 'victim' smoker ought to do nothing and *continue* to smoke (as this would be acting against their own best interests) if he/she wants to be healthy and not die of lung cancer. Be clear though, that there is no moral judgement or blame here. It is simply a case of what is likely to achieve the best outcome for the 'victim' and this is decided on a rational basis.

Notions of 'blame' are simply not part of the 'teleological' approach and are instead associated with a 'deontological' paradigm which sets strict moral rules about right or wrong that are deemed to come from a higher authority (often religion) and are stipulated irrespective of whether they are persuasive, rational or useful. It is deontological (not teleological) paradigms that are concerned with blame, black and white, rigid and inflexible moral judgements.

A 'teleological' approach in relation to self-help looks at all parts of the whole and tries to improve overall effectiveness by considering how useful (or useless) certain mental strategies and behaviours are at achieving peoples' desired outcomes. For example, if your goal is to be physically strong it is not useful (towards achieving your goal/outcome) if you lie about on the couch all day and never strengthen your muscles. On the other hand, when your goal is to relax and rest, lying on the couch is extremely useful and hours can go by in useful pursuit of your goal!

In trying to improve outcomes, a teleological approach looks at 'contributions' towards effectiveness. There is a clear distinction between 'contribution' and 'blame' – they are NOT synonyms and according to any Thesaurus the words are not even roughly similar. For example, if I caught a virus I may have contributed to it getting a stronger hold by working too hard and allowing myself to get overtired but I am not to blame for getting sick. The concept of blame does not even enter into the teleological paradigm and to place 'blame' within in would be a 'category error' (in philosophy terms)!

Going back to our lying on the couch example, a 'deontological' paradigm might set up a moral rule that *people should never be lazy*, resulting in a rigid, moral judgement that lying on the couch is *always* 'lazy', irrespective of its value for relaxing and resting.

It is then only a small step to arguing that some people are *more* 'lazy' than others (or better or superior than others) and people who do not conform to the rigid rules can easily be condemned, punished or ostracised. We currently see much of this conformist behaviour in on-line lynch mobs in social media, who frequently strenuously protect and enforce their rigid moral rules and beliefs through abuse without defensible, rational argument.

Operating (as I do) within a teleological paradigm I am concerned with effectiveness in achieving *outcomes* not with upholding indefensible rules, morality or blame. Within a 'teleological' paradigm it is assumed that we do not have access to the 'absolute' truth but that we are attempting to make the most rational choices we can, given our limited knowledge. As a result, the paradigm is flexible to context with different ways to proceed for different situations. Working out the ways to proceed is on the basis of rational persuasion through argument, without appealing to moral authorities or rigid rules.

With that important point clarified, let's now move onto understanding the four steps of ST and the rational reasons behind them. Of course, if you are not persuaded by the logic or you simply do not care about the consequences of any self-sabotaging behaviour then it is your choice not to follow them. You alone are the author of your own life, and it is you who will experience the consequences and outcomes of your decisions and choices.

STEP ONE: KEEP YOUR BEHAVIOURS USEFUL, EFFECTIVE AND NEVER SELF-SABOTAGING

Following my brief philosophical diversion above, it will come as no surprise that all of your behaviours need to be useful or functional for you and not self-sabotaging. For example, if your anxiety is leading you to drink 15 standard alcoholic drinks per day, then this amount of alcohol will impede your ability to function both at the time of consumption and by giving you a mighty hangover the next day and a lowered mood for several days afterward. It will also inadvertently increase your anxiety as you withdraw and rebound from the sedative effects of ethanol. In the longer term drinking this amount will make it more likely you will develop liver damage, brain damage, chronic sleep problems, dementia, diabetes or various cancers associated with excessive alcohol intake.

Being heavily and regularly inebriated will also create much higher levels of risk in your life which result in serious consequences that you then have to live with. For example, one man I knew *gently* toppled as though in slow motion into a dive over the first-floor stair bannister by simply over-balancing on his descent after about a dozen drinks. He broke his neck and has been lying immobile as a quadriplegic for the past decade: an unbelievably hard way to learn a life lesson.

I have also seen many men in my work who have been punched, stabbed, glassed, and one was blinded during drunken pub brawls where they were the victims of out-of-control drunken perpetrators and in other cases where they themselves were the perpetrators of alcohol-fuelled violence. Many women I have seen also through my work have been raped (and even gang raped) and seriously assaulted while being very drunk.

Even though you may *like* to get blind drunk and you might (rightly) think that you *ought* to be able to get totally legless and still be safe *no matter what*, the reality is that inebriated behaviour is likely to contribute to unwanted outcomes by compromising **your** ability to protect your own interests and be your own best advocate.

Let me explain. Most people in our society behave reasonably and are socialised into civil, co-operative behaviour. As a rule, most people would not rob you, rape you, or kick you in the head and leave you bleeding in the gutter if they came across you when you were heavily inebriated and unable to protect your own interests.

On the other hand, if you were unlucky enough to come across a poorly socialised and opportunistic individual (or gang) who has no qualms about attacking, robbing or taking advantage of your compromised mental state, then your contribution to the equation becomes crucial.

The outcome is likely to depend upon your ability to protect your own interests and the more alcohol you have consumed the less likely it is that you could protect your own interests effectively. While you are clearly not to blame for the incident (obviously the perpetrator is), nevertheless you have contributed to the outcome and your behaviour has not been as useful, functional or in your-own-best-interests, as it could have been.

Step One in ST is all about working out which behaviours in your repertoire serve you well and which behaviours do not serve you well. In this process it is important not to lie to yourself, just because you happen to *enjoy* doing something (like smoking). Nearly all habits feel *enjoyable* once they are established, but that is not, in itself, a good reason for keeping on doing them, especially if they are destructive and are likely to bring you poor outcomes.

One way to help you do this is by locating your behaviours in relation to how other members of society (without the problem) most commonly behave. For example, how much alcohol do most members of society drink? While this will obviously vary from culture to culture, the answer according to the Australian Bureau of Statistics is probably less than two glasses per week per adult on average.

Many 'big' drinkers will most likely be surprised by this figure because over time it comes to *feel* normal to drink 15 glasses of alcohol per day or per week. This is because, once you have been drinking for quite a while the habit becomes established and it then just *feels* normal.

Also, big drinkers tend to hang out with other big drinkers in the same way that smokers tend to hang out with other smokers, skewing their perception of an 'average' intake. This 'hanging out' behaviour allows drinkers and smokers to try and feel 'normal' and pretend they do not have a problem comparative to their peer group. But in ST you will need to be honest with yourself and when you are, I think you will be persuaded that amounts like 15 drinks per day or even per week are neither functional nor common practice. On the other hand, two drinks per week or less (as far as we currently know) probably has fairly minimal consequences.

Let's take a different example of Step One. If you avoid getting on public transport because you feel highly anxious and worry you might have a panic attack in front of everyone, then ask yourself whether avoiding public transport is useful or functional in your life? I think you will find the answer is 'no'.

Not having the option of catching public transport means you probably have to rely on others to give you rides in their car, or you might have to take your own car to places where it is difficult to park. It probably also means that you have to walk or ride your bike instead, and while this is good for exercise it may not always be convenient if it happens to be raining, for example.

Next, ask yourself whether avoiding public transport is self-sabotaging? Again, I think you will find the answer is 'yes'. It limits your freedom, flexibility, options and independence and while you do not overcome your fear of public transport it keeps you forever in a highly anxious state of anticipation of panicking in future scenarios where, for some reason, you might *have* to catch pubic transport.

Then ask yourself whether this is how someone without anxiety in our society would behave? The answer would be a resounding '**no!**' People without anxiety would have the freedom and flexibility to just hop on and off public transport at will, without a care in the world.

So after you have finished this book and you come back to this chapter to start to apply the ST method, you will need to go through all of your problematic behaviours (you know what they are!) and give them the truth test: are they useful or functional for you, are they self-sabotaging, do other societal members without your problem do this behaviour and if so, how much? You can prioritise them so you quit some all at once and others later on if you wish, but make sure you don't forget about the ones further down your list.

These self-sabotaging behaviours that you are going to quit might include all sorts of things. Maybe you exit supermarkets or other places when you feel anxious; perhaps you allow yourself to collapse and become hysterical, irrational and angry when in challenging situations; maybe you don't travel in cars, lifts, aeroplanes, trains or trams in case you have a panic attack; perhaps you don't seek promotion at work, attend interviews, go to social events or do public speaking because you are anxious and afraid of other people judging you badly.

Maybe you waste lots of time doing useless repetitive behaviours like checking switches, locks, taps, numbers or thoughts (needing to have the 'right' thought to somehow keep yourself or others 'safe') or perhaps you refuse to do ordinary and functional behaviours like watching the news or reading the newspaper in case you see something that might inadvertently make you anxious.

Perhaps you wash your hands excessively or wash your clothes excessively or feel you have to keep wiping things clean even though they are already clean. Maybe you struggle to leave the house or go out alone or perhaps you spend hours searching the internet for information about symptoms of imagined catastrophic diseases (like cancer) or perhaps you take your pulse too often and check your breathing to make sure you are not about to faint or have a heart attack or stroke.

Maybe you avoid swimming since you once had a scary incident with the water and allow yourself to visually flashback to or re-play visual images of that scary incident over and over, keeping yourself scared and anxious. Maybe you drink, take drugs or smoke large amounts to try and numb any fear or anxiety. On the other hand, perhaps you allow yourself to lose control and become hysterical at the sight of a tiny little mouse or spider! Whatever, anxiety-driven behaviours you have, you will need to identify them and make a list.

Once you have listed all your problematic behaviours then decide to change them into behaviours that do serve you well. For example, decide to stop or reduce your drinking, or decide to start getting on public transport, or decide to stop washing your hands excessively, or decide to stop checking your pulse or searching the internet for symptoms, or decide to stop mentally replaying flashbacks of past scary events, or decide to start applying for promotions and start learning how to do public speaking! No excuses. I know it sounds simple, **but it really is this simple**!

Forget about deep and complex character traits, forget about difficult subconscious urges, forget about genetic predisposition, forget about difficult personal histories, forget about any other excuses you may have. We can all decide to change our behaviour! If you change your behaviour your brain will change and it will learn to match the new behaviour. Let your brain look after itself. All you have to do is decide to change your behaviour and stick to it.

Although we can all decide to change our behaviour, it nevertheless takes decisiveness. You must be willing to be brave and strong. It is where you must make the *right* decision (for your own interests), not the easier or weaker decision. Not only that, but you need to **commit** to your new behaviour change, for a minimum amount of time, for example, at least two years **before** you re-evaluate it – so you give it a proper chance to see whether and how much it improves your life.

The reason you must commit for a minimum of two years is because although the neural pathways associated with your old self-sabotaging behaviours will have weakened and degraded (and rarely, if ever, give you any trouble), they will not have completely disappeared. While these pathways are still *physically* present (no matter how weakly) they can still be easily re-activated back into your dominant habit.

Don't worry if you struggle changing your behaviours at the start, you will get stronger and it will get easier *very quickly*. But you must be **decisive** – you must refuse to be weak – you must refuse to let yourself lose control by collapsing and going back to your old, unhelpful behaviour. Just put one foot in front of the other each day and keep making yourself stick with the new game plan.

By the way, an *urge* to do an old, useless behaviour *never* has to be acted upon, and if you don't give in to urges or pay any attention to them (more on this in Step Three) they disappear extremely fast. Your new behaviour will quickly become your dominant habit (within hours, days or weeks, depending on *how* decisive you are) and it will become easy to abstain from your old, self-sabotaging habit. The more decisive you are, the less you will tolerate any attentional focus on mentations connected to the old habit and the more it is just like flicking a switch when you quit. Trust me, you can do it – it is all about being *decisive*.

CHAPTER FIVE

STEP TWO: KEEP YOURSELF RELAXED AND ALWAYS BELOW 3/10

This step teaches you just how much mental control you really have over your life. At the heart of this step is the idea that you will *never again* allow yourself to lose control and rise above 3/10 in your agitation level. For your information, 10/10 is the most tense, agitated and anxious you have ever felt and 0/10 is deep internal stillness with no detectable agitation.

To do Step Two properly, it basically means that it does not matter what happens around you – someone may be screaming at you, or there might be 101 things you need to get done, or your boss might be sacking you – still, irrespective of the situation, it is your job to stay internally calm, soft, rational, relaxed and **always** below 3/10.

In short, **never** again give yourself permission to lose control – that is your brief from now on. Commit to this mission. You may have mistakenly thought that losing control helped you at some stage in your earlier life or maybe you thought that you just couldn't help it – you felt so distressed that you just had to blow a gasket one way or another.

When you were younger, perhaps tightening and hardening your body with tension made you feel safer in an unsafe world. Maybe clenching your jaw, hardening your eyes and shutting out scary parts of the world allowed you to feel less vulnerable. Perhaps raising the shoulders, tightening your stomach and retracting the head and neck (like a turtle pulling in under its shell) allowed you to feel more protected and less in danger.

Unfortunately though, tightening and hardening your body physically goes hand in hand with closing and hardening your mind and locking into stubborn mental resistance against things that frighten you.

These 'tension' habits may have once been useful during a difficult childhood where you had to be 'on guard' frequently. Now that you are an adult with a fully developed brain and you are now out of danger and able to be in control of your own life these old tension habits only sabotage you.

Being overly vigilant in your tension level nowadays just wears you out and feels unpleasant, as well as making you respond inappropriately at a level of perhaps 9/10 for problems that only require a 2/10 response. Inappropriate and excessively vigilant responses, as an adult, diminish your level of control in the world since they lead to creating catastrophes where there are none.

These excessive responses easily lead to multiple ways of losing control in life: a bit like winning the battle but losing the war. For example, being terrified of imagined catastrophes might lead to losing control by taking drugs or alcohol or comfort eating to try to block out and numb the feeling of terror. In the short term blocking out the imagined catastrophes might increase feelings of safety and make you think you are winning the battle, but in the end you may lose control of your entire life as these habits or poor 'solutions' become entrenched.

Alternatively, being terrified might lead to a ferocious response of losing your temper and trying to crush your (imagined all-powerful) opponent before they crush you. Again, you may think that in the short term you have won the battle, since your opponent has *appeared* to cave-in. However, in the longer term your opponent will passively block you and refuse to cooperate, making future good outcomes untenable and lowering your levels of real control in the world (see my *Smart Therapy Assertion* booklet for more information on this topic).

In other instances, excessive fear of imagined catastrophes might lead to refusal to do normal, regular behaviours like entering lifts, going into supermarkets, driving the car, flying in planes, going to social events, taking spiders outside, attending work meetings, spending time alone, being independent, attending job interviews, getting on public transport, or touching objects without fear of contamination.

Refusal to engage in the normal range of life activities not only shrinks horizons and makes life concerns more petty, trivial and boring but it also reduces skill development opportunities. Less skill development means lower competency levels compared with other people, making it harder to compete with them for opportunities (like jobs) or resources (like income). Fewer skills also makes coping with normal complex life problems more difficult and frustrating, giving rise to the likelihood of more out-of-control behaviour.

Let's take an example. Let's say you fear to the level of 10/10 the imagined catastrophe of having panic attacks at work. This fear, over time drives you to quit work. Once this happens, you lose opportunities for developing, say IT skills.

On the other hand, others who have been regularly attending work appear competent with their IT skills, and you feel frustrated and 'bad' about yourself in comparison. To counter your sense of inferiority and to express your frustration, you lose control and rant and rave to anyone who will listen about the 'uselessness' of computers and how they are 'taking over' all things human.

This alienates other people who enjoy using computers and find them progressive and helpful tools. Over time, the alienation grows as you further express your 'pet hate' as your skills rapidly diminish in comparison with others.

Gradually, no one wants to hear your complaints anymore and you become more isolated. The more isolated you become the easier it is to employ other out-of-control behaviours like drinking more and more alcohol to comfort yourself in your despair and powerlessness.

Although the details vary, these types of scenarios happen frequently, and I see them over and over in my work every day. People often respond to their hyped-up (10/10) state of anxiety and fear by utilising self-sabotaging escape behaviours. However, escaping (quitting work) only appears to help in the short term, and it can actually result in much larger loses of control (ranting, shutting down, isolation and increased alcohol) over the long term.

Unfortunately, the hyped-up state was the problem at the outset. The imagined 'catastrophe' of having panic attacks at work should never have been allowed to reach 10/10, when it was, in reality 3/10. Had the person maintained their tension level always below 3/10, the whole dreadful scenario would never have happened.

Whatever your situation, losing control does **not** help you now. It keeps you demonstrating over and over to your brain that you are a victim of external events that happen *to you*. Losing control keeps you thinking external stress must necessarily become internal stress, and that you have no control over this transition. Losing control keeps you at 10/10, making continual errors thereafter as a result of excessive hyper-vigilance.

If you keep letting yourself lose control, you remain a puppet on the string of all external stressors and every time you allow yourself to either arc up and lose control or go passive and lose control you are teaching your brain that you are powerless to control your own internal life; that you have no boundaries or separation from the external world. This is simply a myth. At the heart of ST is the power of our prefrontal cortex and using it to **always stay in control**.

It may come as a shock to you, but staying in control, is actually amazingly easy and much of it involves learning a simple exercise, called the 'Body Flop'. Going forward, this exercise will be an important means of always staying in control and less than 3/10 in your tension and agitation level.

The Body Flop only takes about 5 seconds to do so it can be done frequently whenever you feel the need. You can do it sitting down, lying down, standing up or walking around. Other people can't tell you're doing it so feel free to do it absolutely anywhere, anytime. To help you do the Body Flop take a look at this simple brain sketch that I will refer to in the next section.

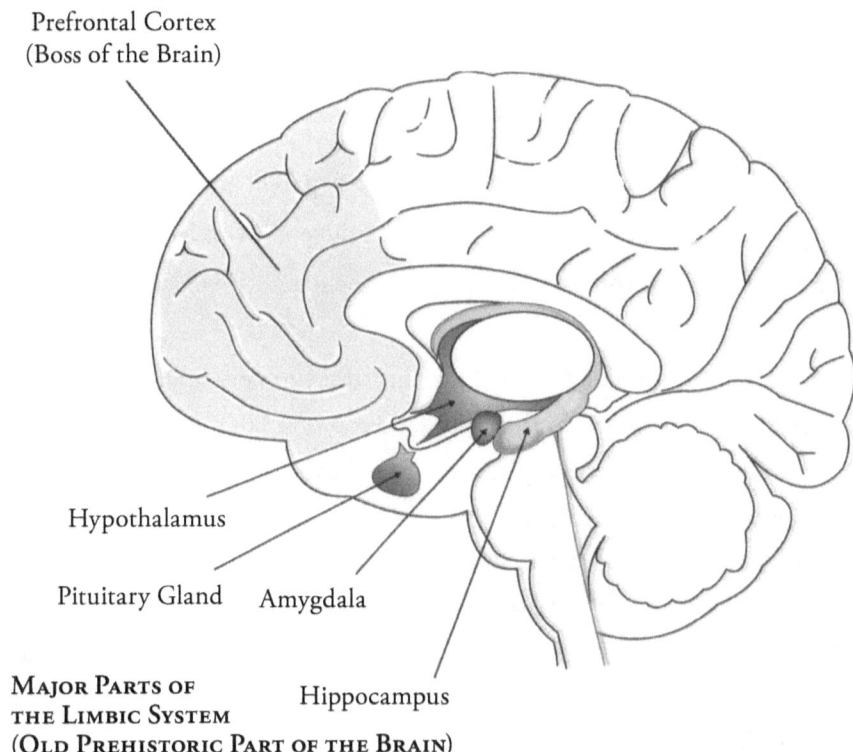

Brain sketch

THE BODY FLOP EXERCISE

To do the Body Flop, there will be three things that you need to do. At first, go slowly and do each part thoroughly. Later as you get more practiced you can do the three aspects as close to simultaneously as you can manage, so that the Body Flop becomes very quick and only takes about 5 seconds to complete. Since the Body Flop exercise is so quick and so effective it can be done many times throughout the day (even 50 or 60 times) without taking up more than a few minutes of your time in total.

FIRST: QUIETEN AND SOFTEN YOUR BRAIN

To help you do this, imagine that you are a parent putting a naughty, chattering child to sleep under the doona or duvet. The parent is (from the diagram above) your prefrontal cortex and the naughty, chattering child is the limbic system.

Remember, from Chapter Two that the limbic system is the old, prehistoric part of the brain that is often responding to threat and danger, producing CRF and generally agitating and creating havoc in the higher brain (your conscious awareness).

Your job as the parent is to soften and quieten it down, patting and dampening it down under the doona until it is quiet and fully calm. Soften it and quieten it. Keep in mind (also from Chapter Two) that the prefrontal cortex (parent) can slow down the firing of these limbic system neurons. The prefrontal cortex has that level of control for you to use if you choose. It only takes a few seconds (at most) to dampen down that chatter. You can actually feel your brain settling, dampening down the chatter and calming right down. Being calm is largely under conscious control.

SECOND: SOFTEN AND FLOP THE ENTIRE BODY

To help you do this allow the body to flop downwards a few centimeters towards the earth imagining that you are releasing every muscle, tendon, ligament, sinew and joint in your body from the top of your head to the bottom of your feet. Allow the whole body to feel warm and comfortable and relaxed and floppy. Imagine that your body is completely soft and free from tension.

Make sure when you 'flop' that you soften the main areas where you, in particular, hold your tension. It may be that you clench your jaw to steel yourself, or raise your shoulders to harden and protect your softer inner core, or perhaps you tighten your eye muscles to keep the world out, or maybe you grip your stomach and tighten your throat to constrict and squash vulnerable feelings.

Most of us have learnt these physical habits of protecting ourselves against the world. So, as the 'flop' moves down your body soften, release and spread these areas, particularly making sure you soften the eyes letting the world enter you freely, drop the shoulders and soften and spread the entire abdomen. Allow every part of your body to be soft and open and so very comfortable.

THIRD: RELEASE ANY FEELINGS OF INNER TENSION AND AGITATION THROUGH THE BREATH

As you know, even though intellectually we are all aware that we *ought* to feel our emotions in our brains, culturally and historically we have located our emotions in our chest and torso, close to our hearts, stomach and other organs. We might feel 'sick to the stomach' from dread or 'heart-broken' from sadness or 'jaundiced about life' (from the liver) or we may 'vent our spleen' with anger.

Fear and the desire to flee is often felt in the chest making us feel 'breathless with fear' and giving us an urge to breathe faster and suck-in large volumes of air to aid our escape. Deep pain, shame and despair are often experienced as a 'lump in the throat' as we try desperately to 'swallow' our pain and 'choke off' our tears.

Yet we don't need to bury any of these emotions no matter how intense they seem to be. We can soften ourselves and let these emotions pass up through us. We don't need to hold them down, festering away in the depths of our guts. They only do us harm when we hold them down tight, never letting them see the light of day. Instead, we can just allow them to come up and simply breathe them out. It feels pleasant to release these intense emotions, so they no longer overwhelm us or trigger us to feel out of control. As we do this we don't even need to know exactly what those feelings are, we can just let them pass through us and simply breathe all of them out together.

All you need to do here in this third part of the Body Flop is a single, long exhalation through your mouth or nose as though you are releasing one long, gentle, soft, stream of air.

As you hold that soft, relaxed stream of breath just imagine that you are letting go of all of your intense feelings through your breath – giving them an airing, letting them be released from the depths of their prison out into the daylight, allowing your body to be set free from all those deep feelings of pain and agitation. As you slowly breathe out, notice how calm you can really feel by freeing those pent-up tensions. Just let yourself be totally rested, warm, comfortable and at peace with yourself.

Even though I have given you quite a bit of detail here for your Body Flop exercise, one of the reasons for this is just to make sure you understand the logic behind each aspect. The other reason is so you can pick out which physical habits, you, as an individual are especially prone to and make sure you particularly soften those areas while doing your Body Flop.

In the end, though, it is just a quick five second exercise of softening and quietening the chattering children; softening and flopping the whole body in a downward wave; and breathing out and freeing any intense emotions through a single, long and soft exhalation.

Once you have practised this exercise slowly several times, then speed it up and start to apply it many times every day. Use the Body Flop exercise every time you reach 3/10 to take you back down to 1–2/10.

At first you probably won't be used to always keeping yourself below 3/10 and taking full responsibility for your own tension levels so you might forget to do your Body Flops frequently enough and then find yourself suddenly and inadvertently reaching 7,8 or 9/10, and feeling very out of control.

Remember that *feeling* out of control often leads to *behaving* out of control whether that involves panic attacks, refusing to do every day, normal activities like getting in lifts or going to the supermarket or driving yourself to work. Feeling out of control may additionally lead to other self-sabotaging behaviours like screaming, hitting, binge eating, excessive alcohol or drug consumption, self-harm, smoking or *punishing* exercise and eating routines, like starvation (in a desperate attempt to regain control following a 'binge').

Recall, that it is **your** job to stay in control so if you find that you have risen in your agitation level then you will need to do a whole series of Body Flops to get your agitation level back down to below 3/10, since each Body Flop is so quick it will probably only bring you down 1–2 points.

If necessary, to help you remember to do Body Flops, attach them to activities that you do regularly throughout the day. For example, do the Body Flop every time you 'save' on your computer, or have a drink or eat or go to the bathroom. When you are first learning to always stay below 3/10, set a timer every twenty minutes to remind you that it is time to do your next Body Flop.

Even though over time you will get much better at just automatically staying below 3/10 in every situation, there will still be times where events are particularly challenging and you need to do a few Body Flops in a row to maintain your composure. My advice is that it is a good idea to always retain this Body Flop exercise throughout your life as an everyday tool even if later on you are so relaxed that you only need to use it occasionally.

LET'S 'GET REAL' ABOUT ANXIETY SO WE CAN CALM DOWN

Often when anxious people come to see me at my work I do the 'Get Real' exercise with them. I first of all ask them to score how anxious they normally feel out of ten. Their answers are often along the lines of 'I feel over 10/10 – maybe 100/10' and when I say 10/10 is the highest score they can have, then they usually say something like 'OK then, but I am *definitely* 10/10 nearly all the time'.

So, I ask them to consider a few scenarios. I ask them how anxious they would feel if they were forced to spend the rest of their lives in prison because they had been wrongly accused of a crime and found guilty. Mostly people say that being innocent and having to go to gaol never to be released would be a clear 10/10.

Then I ask anxious people to consider another situation, where they are held captive by terrorists as some sort of political prisoner and subjected to systematic torture: electric shocks, near drowning in buckets of water, severe sleep deprivation, fingernails ripped out, teeth pulled out and excruciating pain from beatings or whippings.

Then I ask anxious people, which is worse, life-time imprisonment or systematic torture with no clear end. People invariably choose torture as being 10/10, which means life imprisonment has to now be scored lower, usually about 8/10.

Next, I ask people how anxious they would feel if they were facing their own imminent death, for example, if they were in a plane and it was clearly going down and they were sure they would be dead in a minute or two. No one I have seen has ever scored this above systematic torture. So far, I have never had an exception to systematic torture being scored as 10/10.

There is slight variation on how people score life imprisonment versus imminent own death. Some people score it above life imprisonment (so life imprisonment moves to 7/10 and own imminent death goes to 8/10) and others score their own imminent death as 7/10 (since they feel they might be able to 'accept' their own death if they knew there was nothing they could do about it) and therefore, life imprisonment would remain scored at 8/10.

In the end, what I am trying to achieve with this exercise, is the willingness to *differentiate* between challenging events by engaging the frontal brain to rationally and logically judge and assess scenarios instead of allowing the pre-historic limbic system to go into outright catastrophe and run the show.

When people have come from difficult backgrounds, their old limbic system has been in charge too often. Remember, that in ST we are trying to get the frontal brain with its rational, measured and objective capabilities to be in control all the time. To this end, I explain to anxious people that I have seen other people in my work who have survived these sorts of atrocities, particularly refugees from war-torn countries who have often been imprisoned, systematically tortured and raped, and faced severe life-threatening events. Amazingly, in these periods of extreme hardship many of them have been able to exercise high levels of frontal brain control which has helped them survive.

Nevertheless, often in my clinic when we look at events like imprisonment, systematic torture or facing our own death people think these are unlikely events, but actually their everyday equivalents are with us as more often than you might think. Elderly people with declining mobility can find themselves confined and 'imprisoned' within their own homes or in old-age institutions; people with extremely painful diseases like cancer or others with unyielding arthritic conditions can find themselves 'tortured' by ongoing severe pain; and, in the end, we all have to face our own deaths.

So, in a way these events can become markers for just how difficult things can **actually** become in life, and when anxious people come properly to terms with this, they are generally able to score their own anxiety at more realistic levels like 3/10. Given these markers of how hard life can get, I ask people to desist from using inflammatory words and to 'get real' from now when they describe their levels of stress. No more 'OMG! That anxiety was hideous!' You will see from Step Three in the next chapter that what I ask for is no words at all about anxiety and indeed complete indifference to their 'relatively' mild levels of distress.

THE WHATEVER HAPPENS EXERCISE ALSO CALMS US DOWN

This next exercise is somewhat counter-intuitive, but I often get anxious people to try it because it helps weaken the over-reaction of the limbic system, thereby taking the fuel out of anxiety and assisting in always remaining below 3/10.

For this exercise, I ask people to tell me what they are scared will happen when they become anxious. Sometimes people are frightened they will be negatively scrutinised by others, other times they are anxious they will go mad, or develop a terrible life-threatening disease, or that their anxiety 'symptoms' will never stop, or that they will suddenly vomit, urinate or faint in public. We all have great imaginations!

Once I know what really frightens people, then I might build it into a 'defiance' and 'tempting fate' exercise where I explicitly describe the main aspects of their fear fully and comprehensively and place it into a framework that anxious people memorise and say out aloud to themselves a few times a week, preferably in front of the mirror (to increase the effect).

The basic framework looks like this:

'Whatever happens, happens … So be it if I … So be it if I … So be it if I … I'll deal with it, I'll manage, I'll cope. In fact, **bring it on** – Come on anxiety, **go your hardest**, do your worst, **give it everything you've got**! Come on anxiety – make me … !'

Just before I go ahead and fill in the detail of this exercise, I want to explain my approach a little more clearly in relation to the content of fear themes and whether or not it is appropriate to use this exercise. There are some fear themes where I don't use this exercise as it might appear to be sending the wrong message. For example, I never use this exercise when people are anxious that they will hurt others perhaps physically or sexually.

Even though, in my experience, people who are anxious about hurting others are the **least** likely of anyone to harm other people I don't ever want to appear to encourage harm towards others, even within the almost 'mocking' tone of this exercise since there is nothing remotely funny about physical or sexual abuse. Yet from a purely theoretical perspective this exercise could be used and may assist in recovery.

For your information, the reason that anxious people are the least likely of anyone to harm others is precisely because people develop *the exact* fear that terrifies them, that is the most abhorrent to them and where they could not imagine anything worse.

In fact, in 20 years of clinical work every person that I have seen who is frightened of hurting other people has been highly and *overly* morally rigorous. In fact, it is likely that it is their *excessive* moral rigidity that has led them to develop their fear of harming others.

When you think about it this is not surprising. If we developed fears that didn't really scare us, people would not give two hoots about them and there would be no anxiety to correct in the world. In contrast, I have found in my work that each person develops the fear they, as an individual, are most terrified of experiencing.

Anxious people often say to me that they 'wished' they had someone else's fear because it would be 'so much easier' to get rid of than the fear they experience. The bottom line, is that we have each built our own individual brain and, whatever scares us most, will (unfortunately) be the content of our fear theme should we develop anxiety.

Where fear themes are not about hurting others, still the concepts can be quite alarming to anxious people. To counter this, in setting up this exercise I try to capture the absolute 'worst' outcomes of their fear that could be imagined (giving exaggerated versions of the fear theme) and this slightly 'mocks' or makes fun of the fear. This brings the anxious person fully into contact with the details of their fear theme, but the slight mockery helps with not overly alarming them.

I will give a few examples of how this framework might be filled in. Let's say you were frightened of dying via sudden death or developing cancer or another disease. The framework would be completed something like this:

'Whatever happens, happens ... So be it if I have a heart attack or stroke and keel over tomorrow. So be it if I develop a brain tumour and go "gaga". So be it if I get MS or motor neuron disease, I'll deal with it, I'll manage, I'll cope. In fact, **bring it on** – Come on, anxiety **go your hardest**, do your worst, **give it everything you've got**! Come on anxiety make me **drop dead**!'

On the other hand, if the fear theme was one of going mad, the framework might be completed like this:

'Whatever happens, happens ... So be it if I go stark raving mad and start howling at the moon tonight. So be it if the whole world thinks I'm totally crazy and paranoid. So be it if I start cackling away at my imagined voices and have to be involuntarily admitted to a psychiatric unit I'll deal with it, I'll manage, I'll cope. In fact, **bring it on** – Come on, anxiety **go your hardest**, do your worst, **give it everything you've got**! Come on anxiety make me **go mad**!'

Alternatively, if the person was afraid of the negative judgement and scrutiny of others, the framework might be completed as follows:

'Whatever happens, happens ... So be it if the whole world is laughing uproariously right now at my entire life. So be it if I am judged to be the biggest idiot nob ever to have breathed air in the entire universe. So be it if every person on the planet thinks I am a complete loser, I'll deal with it, I'll manage, I'll cope. In fact, **bring it on** – Come on, anxiety **go your hardest**, do your worst, **give it everything you've got**! Come on anxiety, make me look **utterly ridiculous**!'

Where the fear was one of suddenly vomiting, fainting or urinating in public the framework might look like:

'Whatever happens, happens ... So be it if I projectile vomit across the meeting room today. So be it if I pass out soon afterwards and wet my pants all over the place. So be it if I look totally gross, ugly, spewy and incontinent, I'll deal with it, I'll manage, I'll cope. In fact, **bring it on** – Come on, anxiety **go your hardest**, do your worst, **give it everything you've got**! Come on anxiety, make me **piss my pants**!'

Notice that in this exercise I also specify a time that is either in the present or close to the present time, in order to make it more immediate and real. For example, the person might: keel over *tomorrow* with a heart attack; or be howling at the moon *tonight*; or projectile vomit *today*, or have the world laughing at them *right now*.

There is another context where I would not use this exercise, and that is where people are terrified that someone close to them will come to harm or die. This is **not** because saying out aloud 'Come on anxiety make **Janice die**!' is going to have any bearing whatsoever on whether or not Janice 'dies'; rather it is because I find that people are generally still too superstitious (even in modern Western society) to explicitly 'tempt fate' to this degree, even in mockery.

Worse still, if 'Janice' did happen to inadvertently have an accident or die around the time of doing this exercise, even though it would have been a complete coincidence, the anxious person might never forgive themselves and I would never want that to happen.

Again though, from a purely theoretical perspective this exercise could be used in that context and may assist in recovery. Despite these caveats, I still include this Whatever Happens exercise because with many people it is incredibly effective in immediately getting rid of their limbic, CRF-fuelled anxiety.

With my own anxiety I was initially (in my very early 20's) frightened of things like having a heart attack (following my father's unexpected death from a cardiac event), but a couple of years later my fear theme morphed from the body to the brain. I remember suddenly being terrified that I would somehow 'lose my mind' and 'go mad'. (For your information, it is very common for fear themes to become like moving targets where the fear theme shifts to related concepts. This occurs simply because neurons are connected to each other and related synapses and the themes within them are easily retrieved by paying excessive attention on one neural population which then activates a downstream neural population of laterally-related synapses.)

When my fear theme morphed, I used to find it extremely difficult to go to sleep because I was scared that letting my mind relax just before falling asleep might allow it to enter into unrestrained 'madness' territory and make me more likely to go psychotic. Yet on the other hand, I knew that I needed to relax my mind in order to fall asleep.

This was a catch-22 and it meant that I was often badly sleep-deprived during those years. I thought that the only thing preventing me from going mad was my hypervigilance at keeping control over my thoughts, and to this end, I would constantly 'jolt' myself awake at the first signs of mental relaxation and sleep onset. When awake, I would then mentally scan vigilantly for any 'strange' voices or 'mad' thoughts.

For some unknown reason, it occurred to me one day to try and do the exact opposite of what I was doing. Obviously 'jolting' myself awake constantly and mentally scanning for 'mad' thoughts was not a good long-term solution, so trying the opposite seemed like a good idea at the time. Amazingly, even in its infant form, this Whatever Happens exercise, immediately took the fuel out of my anxiety.

Doing this exercise demonstrated to me that I could let go the 'brakes' and the constant paying of attention via hypervigilant mental scanning for any 'mad' thoughts and, I could even go so far as to fully and comprehensively *welcome in* the 'madness' and *defiantly* tempt fate, and yet I still did **not** actually go mad. This immediately took away the power of my anxiety (physiologically, it would have reduced the number of agitated, firing neurons related to my fear theme), which enabled me to pay my anxiety less attention.

I recall that at the time, all of this was extremely counter-intuitive (I had no-one guiding me and I had not yet developed anything of ST) but I was amazed at how effortlessly this exercise evaporated my anxiety, allowing me to feel calm and in control and below 3/10. When I felt this calm, there was no longer any need to pay attention to my fear theme – so it simply disappeared!

I would definitely recommend trying this Whatever Happens exercise even if it feels quite counter-intuitive since it so powerfully demonstrates that even with practically *begging* yourself to do whatever you are afraid of, the fearful event still doesn't happen, allowing you to feel more mentally relaxed (below 3/10) and thereby making it so much easier to stop paying constant and hypervigilant attention to your fear theme going forward.

Finally, just to remind you, Step Two has been about reducing physiological agitation and tension and then keeping it low. If there are other relaxation methods you prefer to use that will keep you below 3/10 then by all means use them. In this chapter I have given you some methods that many anxious people find particularly helpful, but please employ other methods (like deep rhythmic breathing or meditation) if you find them beneficial.

The crucial message in Step Two is to be realistic about where your anxiety sits in relation other markers of how bad life can actually be (gaol, torture or death) and to remove any fuel you can from your anxiety (with the Whatever Happens exercise) so there is less physiological pressure to pay it attention.

Finally, on a minute-to-minute basis every day ensure that you

always stay relaxed and in control and **never** allow yourself to lose control again (use the Body Flop exercise, anywhere, anytime). Remember to be very clear about this: It is **your** job, **your** responsibility, not matter what is happening around you, to ensure that you will never again rise above 3/10.

CHAPTER SIX

STEP THREE: NEVER ALLOW YOURSELF TO PAY ATTENTION TO *EVEN A SINGLE* SELF-SABOTAGING MENTATION *EVER AGAIN!*

This might sound like an impossible goal to many people, especially those who have been ruminating for perhaps ten hours every day for years. But in reality, it is actually completely within your ability to achieve this. Not only is it achievable, but you can learn to do it almost immediately.

Often people think that their sensations, feelings, thoughts, memories or images just take them over – as though they have no control over their own mentations. This is simply untrue and probably arises from cultural, historical and religious notions that we have a mind that somehow stretches beyond the material basis of our brain and (within religion) leads us to concepts of 'soul'.

This type of thinking leads us to assume that the mind is somehow 'unknowable', wrapped in mystery and mystique. Yet, as far as we know through science, there is fairly minimal mystique, with the mind simply being a manifestation or outward expression of brain processes over which we can exert extremely high levels of control.

Please let me explain, with a quick exercise. Place both of your hands flat in front of you on a table. Choose to pay attention to lifting the index finger of your dominant hand. Lift it up. Then choose to stop lifting your index finger and allow it to fall back down onto the table. As you do this exercise say to yourself 'lift it, stop it, lift it, stop it' as your finger lifts up and down.

Do this exercise several times, then shift to the index finger on your non-dominant hand and repeat the exercise. Again, say 'lift it, stop it, lift it, stop it' as your finger moves up and down. Notice that *even* with your non-dominant hand (unless you have an injury or disability), you have 100% control over lifting or stopping lifting your finger. The choice is yours to make – do you lift it or do you stop lifting it? This is what you might describe as a 'body' behaviour. That is, our neural activity and precision within our brains at lifting or stopping lifting is outwardly expressed in our body (index finger).

Thoughts, feelings, imagery, sensations, and memories are also outward expressions of our brain's neural activity and precision, it is just that they are expressed within the brain or mental sphere (mind) rather than the body. As such these mentations can be called brain 'behaviours' or mental 'behaviours' – but they are still no less behaviours than moving our finger.

Just like any other behaviour, we have 100% control about how we intervene. Basically, whether they be body or brain behaviours, our brains can exert exactly the same level of control and precision. We can choose to lift the index finger or we can choose to stop lifting it, or we can choose to pay attention to self-sabotaging thoughts and feelings or we can choose not to pay attention to them. The choice is ours to make. There is actually very little mystery.

Knowing this, helps us to be clear about exactly how we ought to respond to unwanted mentations. Step Three is all about deciding which thoughts, images, sensations, feelings, or memories you want more of, and which ones you would prefer became a smaller (or non-existent) part of your awareness. For you to be able to achieve Step Three easily, I need to give you a bit more precise information to help you understand exactly what you need to do.

THE DIFFERENCE BETWEEN 'FOCUSED' AND 'PERIPHERAL' ATTENTION

It is crucial that you understand the difference between 'focused attention' and 'peripheral attention' or awareness. To do this, imagine that you are sitting in a room having a vigorous conversation with another person. You are chatting back and forth, asking questions, laughing, interrupting each other, reading each other's body language and facial expressions, remembering details told to you, and you are both adding relevant little bits and pieces to the conversation to expand it.

Think of your 'focused' attention as being like a *direct line* between yourself and the object you are paying a high level of attention to, in this case, the person you are conversing with. There is no obvious interruption to that direct line – it is like a projection that travels from your head to their head.

We know that our focused attention is quite singular, and that humans are very poor at focusing our attention on more than one thing at any one time. Remember from Chapter Two that focused attention is highly distinctive in the brain and can be detected easily as synchronous firing. Focused attention is like we are applying effort to study an object in a singular and disciplined way.

However, while having that vigorous conversation you still have some peripheral attention – that is, you might have vague awareness of traffic sounds coming from out on the street, or you might have a vague sense of smelling some food cooking out in the kitchen somewhere, or you might be vaguely aware that there is a bookcase over on the other side of the room, or you might have a vague awareness that your dog still needs to be fed, or a vague awareness that you are feeling a bit cold. This is your peripheral awareness, and you can think of it as vaguely out to the sides of your focused attention and perhaps behind your own head.

We know from research that people are highly efficient at learning whatever material is in our focused attention, whereas we only lay down information from our peripheral attention very weakly (and often, not at all). The more we have immersed our full focused attention on the vigorous conversation, then the less we will recollect material from those peripheral sources. We also know from research that any peripheral material we have inadvertently laid down at a neural level is lost from our memories very easily.

For example, let's say you walk 3 kilometres to work each day and you have worked at the same job for the past five years. Over that time you will have walked the same route there and back numerous times. Yet if I were to ask you what was the paint colour of the fourth house on the right of the fifth block of your walk you would almost certainly be unable to tell me despite having walked past it over three thousand times – unless there had been some *specific reason* for you to pay it focused attention.

This is because that house was only in your peripheral attention and not in your focused attention. If, on the other hand your brand new shiny car happened to be the same colour as that house and you noticed it and paid it focused attention then you would remember the house paint colour without any difficulty.

In other words, we learn, remember and retrieve material with ease from our focused attention, whereas we generally fail to learn, fail to remember and therefore fail to retrieve material gleaned from our peripheral attention.

Understanding this point is crucially important to the ST method, because it allows us to exploit these learning processes to our full advantage by shifting unwanted mentations into our peripheral attention, thereby fostering their dissolution.

WHICH MENTATIONS TO KEEP AND WHICH TO REMOVE?

First of all, imagine you have a magic wand. If you could, what would you remove from your mental experience and what would you increase in your mental experience?

Many people initially answer this question by saying 'I just want to be happy all the time'. Fair enough, but there are three main problems with this answer. Firstly, happiness is actually a vague and imprecise concept, and what makes one person happy makes another person miserable.

Secondly, it is totally unrealistic to want to be happy all the time since no one can possibly be, unless we are brain dead (and not even then). This is basically, because, like all animals, humans are highly responsive to our environment, and *difficult* things happen in that environment that we must deal with if we are to keep living.

Often things that happen make us sad or *very* sad and indeed they *ought* to make us sad. We would lack all empathy (for ourselves and others) if that were not the case. Life creates many obstacles for all us that we must struggle to overcome – this is simply an inevitable consequence of life. We are in some sort of denial of reality if we cannot accept inevitable hardships in life.

Thirdly, 'I just want to be happy all the time' is like a child's demand, and it actually arises from a victim perspective of down deep not believing we can cope with adversity. We may have learnt as children that we could not cope with adversity, but once we are adults we are more than up to the task.

The key here is not to deny or try to get rid of the adversity but to insist on dealing with it *constructively*. In my experience from my work it is the destructive and self-sabotaging ways that people deal with adversity that is the problem rather than the adversity itself.

So, when I ask the magic wand question in my work, I am looking for a more precise answer than general 'happiness'. When pushed to be specific most people say they want to experience fewer catastrophic, worrying, anxious, angry, depressive, self-depreciating, addictive, psychotic, and fixated thoughts, feelings, images, sensations or memories.

People also report that they want to have more calm, constructive, kind, friendly, humorous, rational and optimistic mentations. When pushed to be even more precise most people generally do not want to give up their deeply human capacity for sadness, particularly when it is appropriate and when it is dealt with constructively.

Now that we are getting much more specific, our aims become much more realistic. We have now identified the exact categories of mentations we want to have more of and the mentations of which we want fewer.

The next stage though is that our answers to the magic wand question ought to change from words such as 'like' and 'want' to words such as 'intend' or 'ensure'. Words such as 'like' and 'want' are associated with a child's demand that lacks the power to make events happen, and reflects the emotionally-driven, primitive limbic system of the brain. Instead, let's change the statement to: We have now identified exactly which mentations we *intend* to have more of and the mentations of which we *intend* to have fewer.

Now the statement moves closer to matching our true level of brain control since when we *intend* to do something we assume we have the power and control to **make** it happen. This is an important distinction in the way you understand and comprehend ST.

Of course, even though having fewer worrying, anxious, depressive, angry, catastrophic, self-depreciating, addicted, psychotic, or fixated thoughts and feelings will inevitably increase your overall 'happiness' level that was *not* actually the aim. If your goal was purely to achieve 'happiness', then every time you felt *legitimately* sad you would see that as a failing to achieve your goal.

Instead, the goal here is to build a brain that is packed full of highly constructive approaches, tools and strategies that help solve life's obstacles, and even though that brain will (inadvertently) be happier, it will also be capable of deep levels of sorrow and sadness when this is appropriate, necessary and useful (more on this later).

To achieve this outcome, it all boils down to one rule of thumb: Any mentation you intend to increase in your brain ought to get lots of focused attention, whereas any sensation, feeling, thought, image or memory that you intend to decrease in your brain ought not receive any focused attention at all – literally, *not even a second* of your time.

Worrying, becoming anxious and catastrophic, mental scanning of fear themes, mental scanning of physical sensations of anxiety, getting angry and bitter, putting yourself and others down, focusing on substances of addiction, having anxious, fixated and self-depreciating thoughts and feelings all hold you back and stop you progressing in life. It is all too easy to become overly-focused on these internal ruminations instead of paying attention to learning the necessary skills to move through life more effectively.

HOW DO I DO STEP THREE EXACTLY?

To achieve Step Three, you will learn to move any anxious, destructive and self-sabotaging mentations out of your focused attention and into your peripheral attention. This applies equally for *all* mentations, including sensations, feelings, thoughts, images or memories. You will imagine 'sliding' or 'slipping' the destructive and self-sabotaging mentations off to the side, out and away from the direct line of your focused attention.

You will know when a destructive thought is arising from your limbic system into your frontal, conscious brain because it is almost always accompanied by intense and unpleasant sensations (like nausea, sweating, blushing or dizziness) or by unpleasant feelings (like fear, dread, hostility, anxiety, fury, shame, humiliation, rage, or intense stress). Many people describe the surfacing of destructive mentations as being like a 'wave' that is unmistakable, all-encompassing and floods them with intense emotion.

Since this 'wave' of intense feelings and sensations is unmistakable, it is your cue to immediately slide or slip all of it out into your periphery. Any mentation in any way associated with the intense 'wave', like visual images, or old bits of memory, as well as the feeling itself, goes off to the side and out of your focused attention. Pay it not a shred of attention. Try not to wait for the full conscious experience of the thought. For example, if you have an intense sensation (of increased heart rate) and a simultaneous feeling (say, of dread) suddenly come upon you and you 'sense' that the thought that will accompany that 'wave' is 'OMG! I'm sure I'm going to panic', slip it off at the point of 'OM ...' while it is still *half-formed*.

If you do not slide self-sabotaging mentations away immediately, they will 'stick' (as they become more fully formed thoughts, images or memories) in your focused attention and even though you still have the brain power to slide them off to the side, it is harder to do so. One thought easily leads to another, which leads to another. It is much easier to slip them into the periphery while they are still sensations and feelings and half-formed thoughts, **before** you have more solidly fixed your attention onto them.

Remember, that initially your brain will apply pressure for you to focus your attention on these unwanted mentations – they will feel *compelling*. This happens for two reasons. Firstly, because your brain has been in the habit of paying attention to these useless mentations in the past, it has learnt that it ought to continue to do so in case there really is any threat or danger. Secondly, these mentations can be very intense and numerous (from CRF-fuelling) so they can easily capture the attentional processes in your frontal brain.

Be clear though, and make sure you don't fall for it! Remember, this is no different to lifting or not lifting the index finger: You have 100% control over what you choose to bring into your attentional focus. **Use that power!**

It is important in the ST process however, that you do not exert highly forceful mental effort trying to eradicate unwanted mentations by becoming didactic and saying things to yourself like 'I must get rid of that thought'. Self-sabotaging thoughts do **not** have to be eradicated. Indeed, forceful mental effort might be inclined to rally brain processes to pay further attention. In ST there is no need whatsoever to be forceful about self-sabotaging mentations since they do not need to be eradicated. They only need to be slipped <u>gently</u> off into the periphery with barely any effort.

In ST I have found that the best way to do this is to show a complete *lack* of interest in the unwanted thought, thereby trivialising it. As you slip the self-sabotaging thought off to the side it might help you initially to say things like: 'what a completely uninteresting and boring thought', or 'who could be bothered with such a tedious and silly thought', or 'how dull and wearisome', or 'go your hardest you moronic and boring thought', or 'bring it on you bore, as if I haven't heard that one before'. As time goes by though, it is enough to just mentally wave-off the useless mentations without any internal commentary.

Showing no interest whatsoever requires very little effort, so sliding self-sabotaging mentations off becomes much easier (and even enjoyable!) rather than struggling against them or trying to get rid of them. After slipping them into your periphery they will probably still try to come back quite a lot to begin with, but so long as you continue with showing complete disinterest, disregard, and disdain for them – slipping them off before they 'stick' – they will give up and start to dramatically reduce within days and hardly be there at all after a few weeks.

As you continue to slip self-sabotaging mentations from your focussed attention, in the ensuing months you may still have some sense that they are vaguely out there somewhere in the 'ether' of your periphery. Don't be even remotely concerned about this. Be assured that the relevant synapses are rapidly degrading and breaking apart from lack of use.

With this synaptic degradation, mentations quite rapidly become fewer and fewer until you rarely (if ever) experience them again. Even though the change occurs by small increments and is not hugely obvious day to day, strangely, in a couple of years, you will look back at yourself and be at a loss to understand how you could have possibly taken your own anxiety so seriously.

SOME TYPES OF MENTATIONS YOU MIGHT DECIDE TO SLIP OFF INTO THE PERIPHERY

Sensations to remove could include: vague feelings of faintness, nausea, weak legs, increased heart rate, clamminess, blushing, tingling, sweats, shakes, tinnitus, butterflies, agitation, tension, stress, or 'jolting' alertness.

Feelings to be slipped off may include: dread, hypervigilance, powerlessness, flat mood, alarm, trepidation, terror, fear, panic, collapse, awfulness, shock, derealisation (disconnection), disgust, excessive caution, horror, inertia, apathy, lethargy, unwillingness, stubbornness, inflexibility, obstinacy, distress, disturbance, doom and gloom, anger, rage, fury, intolerance, envy, global guilt/self-condemnation, hatred, impatience, mean-spiritedness, or hostility.

Images to be slipped off may include: frightening visual images of past traumas (often called 'flashbacks'), scary images of things like seeing blood, images of self-harm, violent images, images seeing yourself 'collapse' under threat, images that degrade or harm other people (like violent sexual imagery often encountered in pornography and then internalised), images of yourself not coping in various situations, images of yourself shaking, trembling and crumbling, or masochistic images.

Memories to be slipped-off into the periphery would include any memories that are self-sabotaging and undermine your ability to currently see yourself as a highly competent person. For example, slip-off any memories of past failures, past embarrassments, past shames, past capitulations, or past collapses and memories of being powerless. Keep them out of your focussed attention until they have faded sufficiently (as the devoted synapses break apart from lack of re-visiting). Later, once you have developed more mental control skills in ST, then, if it will benefit you, you can analyse these memories constructively from an emotional distance and learn from them.

The types of **thoughts** that might be removed could include: catastrophic thoughts ('this is the worst thing *ever*' or 'OMG I would literally die if that happened'); or what ifs (running through worse case scenarios endlessly and trying to plan so they don't eventuate like 'what if I panic'); anticipatory worry (worrying in advance of an event); or collapse thoughts like 'why bother' or 'this is too hard' or 'what's the point' which coincide with feelings of collapse and powerlessness making it harder to become an active self-agent.

Similarly, distress intolerance thoughts ought to be slipped off into the periphery as well. These include thoughts like 'I can't stand it' or 'I've got to get out of here **now**' or 'I can't bear it' which all coincide with exiting behaviour. If there is one thing you don't want to do, it is leaving a situation when you are panicking and have not yet gained proper mental control over the situation. Instead stay, calm down to below 3/10, slip off all distress intolerance thoughts and once you are fully calm and have done what you came for, then you can leave.

Thoughts that support anger, hostility, envy, hatred, inflexibility, rigidity, rage, meanness, excessive caution, obstinacy, derealisation, intolerance, global guilt/self-condemnation (see next section), racism, sexism, ageism, impatience, stubbornness, fury, cruelty, heartlessness, or apathy are also best slipped off into the periphery, since over time, these mentations just eat us from the inside out turning us into bitter, twisted, unfulfilled versions of ourselves when we could have been so much kinder, productive, and given so much more love in the world.

Other thoughts like global condemnation might also be slipped off the repertoire. Global condemnation is where you make statements about yourself or others that wipe you or them out in one stroke, like: 'I'm hopeless', 'I'm useless', 'he/she is a waste of space', 'I'm bad', 'he's a cretin', 'she/he's a loser', 'she's a slag/slut/mole/bitch/cunt', 'I'm ugly', 'he/she is a nigger/boong/chink/ape/neanderthal', 'she/he is stupid', 'I'm a bad mother', 'he/she is an idiot' or 'I'm a moron'.

The problem with these global statements is that they are inaccurate (no one is totally bad or stupid or useless or ugly). Global statements when used on others tend to place them into these irredeemable global 'categories' from which it is nearly impossible to escape. For example categories like 'cunts, sluts, boongs, idiots or losers' are pretty much universally held in contempt and 'half' measures are rarely articulated. It is conceptually more difficult to be half a slut, half a Neanderthal, half a loser, half a cunt or half stupid.

These global condemnation statements also dismiss other people without reason, allowing the speaker to (unjustifiably) feel smug about themselves in comparison. This smug attitude towards others creates the illusion that the speaker requires no self-critique (since any 'problem' is located in the *other* person who is the 'loser', subtly placing the speaker in the 'winner' position).

Global condemnation statements (also called 'global guilt') when used on the 'self' are equally problematic. Any statement that is all-encompassing makes it difficult to know where to start to fix it up. It feels too overwhelming. Allowing ourselves to have these global thoughts is actually a strategy to *let ourselves completely off the hook*, so we don't have to critique ourselves in any *specific* way, while at the same time, feeling that we have given ourselves a good 'beating' or 'whipping'.

In reality we have done neither, and following an episode of global self-condemnation people have usually not changed one iota. This is because global thoughts or statements leave us nowhere to move, we are *all* bad, *totally* useless, *completely* stupid, thereby subtly giving no space for small incremental improvement since if we are 100% bad there is no part of us that can be redeemed. This is a subtle sleight of hand that allows *complete evasion* of responsibility while *appearing* to take responsibility.

However there is a cost in using the self-condemnation strategy. By telling ourselves we are completely hopeless/useless/stupid/bad we undermine the cohesion of our sense of self or self-identity, thereby rendering ourselves less able to function or take action on our own behalf. While we are in the total self-condemnation phase we make ourselves more globally passive since we are utterly 'hopeless' and 'useless'.

Since totally dysfunctional, ineffectual and passive people cannot survive for long (if really severe they would be unable to feed or even toilet themselves), people then must (usually quite quickly) flick from self-condemnation into applying a strategy to 'activate' themselves from their created passivity in order to justify and then resume their normal 'default' self-identity.

Most commonly the activation strategy that people use is anger and blame. So they move from 'I'm hopeless'/'I'm useless'/'I'm a loser' into 'she/he is fucked'/'the world is fucked'/'why do I bother'/'I'm just going to do my own thing'. At this point the status quo is resumed and people have evaded responsibility and managed to not reflect at all on their own contribution and have therefore not changed at all.

This whole messed-up, distorted can of worms is evoked fundamentally because when people have come from difficult backgrounds they often hold an (incorrect) assumption that they cannot bear-to consider any self-critique. They believe they cannot survive the distress of self-critique, and that their sense of self would 'collapse' if they accepted any criticism or took responsibility for sometimes being wrong or making errors when contributing to outcomes.

Yet so much misery in the world arises from this one incorrect assumption. It is a main player in overly-zealous defensive strategies, ideological dogmas, closed-mindedness, anger, being overly demanding, stubbornness, closing down, inability to move forward in life, substance abuse, violence, excessive alcohol intake, over-eating, harbouring of resentments and refusal to engage in helpful solutions.

It so often lies at the heart of what leads people to (unnecessarily) take *objective* arguments personally and become deeply and unnecessarily upset, then sulking, storming off, acting out, refusing to listen or escalating or becoming aggressive. All this, because of one wrong assumption that self-critique and the subsequent taking of responsibility would be too much to bear.

Still it is easy to see how it happens. When children are growing up within difficult environments, with many frequently, uncontained stressful life events and they are in the process of building their (often fragile) sense of self, it is easy to see how global condemnation and criticism from others is extremely hard to cope with and leads to the assumption that additional self-reflection and critique could easily destabilise an already compromised structure. Not surprisingly, children from difficult backgrounds learn to overly protect, deflect and defend against proper self-reflection and self-critique.

Sadly, due to our highly efficient brain, once this assumption is established firmly in childhood, it will carry through into adulthood unless critiqued and removed from the repertoire. Yet the assumption itself prevents critique since any critique is deemed dangerous to the fragile sense of self, apparently producing a catch-22.

Fortunately though, we always, as adults (and even as older adolescents) have our frontal brain and mightily powerful prefrontal cortex. We **always** have our free-will to over-ride with logic and rationally any incorrect assumption, and to choose our attentional focus, determining what we will learn and consolidate in our brains, no matter how deeply our assumptions are entrenched.

Of course, it is easy to *not* realise we have this free-will, since difficult backgrounds tend to result in 'reactive' limbic brain dominance causing hyper-vigilance and threat-deterrence (as is sensible and rational in the circumstances), rather than exerting 'proactive' frontal brain engagement that is (in evolutionary terms) a luxury reserved for times without threat. However, once we know that we can recruit our frontal brain at any time with highly effective results, *then* we can act in our own and others' best interests and learn to reflect properly on ourselves and take responsibility for outcomes.

So while global self-condemnation and global guilt are basically a way of letting ourselves off the hook, specific self-critique is crucially important and needs to be done more often than most people currently think necessary. There is such a strong view amongst mental health professionals that we ought to be unswervingly positive about ourselves to overcome past trauma and to build self-esteem.

In my view this is completely incorrect. It is not a question of critique or not critique, but rather a question of how we do it. Global self-condemnation is both destructive to self-identity unless paired with an activating strategy (like anger or blame) and, it results in no change and no taking of responsibility. On the other hand, specific self-critique is constructive, results in incremental improvement and change, and leads to taking proper responsibility.

Specific self-critique looks like this: Yesterday I behaved badly. I was too harsh with Jenny when she needed my kindness. That wasn't fair of me. I think it might have happened because I was over-tired and feeling a bit strung out, like I had to 'harden' myself to get through the day. Next time I am tired I will make sure I remember to go softer rather than harder, to be kinder and not feel I have to become harsh and brittle. I will also try to get less tired by getting to bed earlier when possible, say by 9.30 pm. I will also remember to apologise to Jenny when I see her tomorrow.

Notice in specific self-critique, that I am specific about **when** and **how** I behaved badly (yesterday, and by being too harsh when Jenny needed my kindness), and I am not bad (global) rather I *behaved badly in a specific instance* (which we all do from time to time). I then consider **why** my poor behaviour might have happened (I was over-tired) and I decide to **change my behaviours** in future (get to bed earlier when possible, go softer rather than harder if I am over-tired, and apologise to Jenny).

Since global condemnation is really just a strategy to avoid taking responsibility, what we use instead in ST is **large amounts** of specific self-critique. By applying specific self-critique we teach our brains that we can quite easily (contrary to past assumptions) cope with self-critique and, in fact, it keeps us moving on and constantly learning in a constructive manner. And, if there is one thing we want to do in life it is keep all our pieces (of self) moving forwards because when they get stuck – that's when we shut down!

In the end though, Step Three, has one over-riding rule: Pay attention **only** to **constructive** mentations and stop paying any attention at all to destructive mentations. Initially you may intend to stop paying any attention at all to anything that is in any way related to your anxiety. That is a good way to start: **Not a single mentation in any way connected to anxiety gets attention.**

However, later on and with a more sophisticated understanding of ST you can be more subtle in your thinking and realise you can still think about anxiety but only in an abstracted way, specifically, **only** in a constructive manner. For example, you can consider how to solve it or think about theories related to anxiety; but you can **never** immerse in the hypervigilant limbic system *experience* of anxiety again. Make sure you understand the difference!

CHAPTER SEVEN

STEP FOUR: KEEP SHIFTING YOUR ATTENTION 100% ONTO CONSTRUCTIVE ACTIVITIES

When I talk about constructive activities I mean any activity that **progresses** you or improves you in your life. A constructive activity is never self-sabotaging and includes many different types of actions, some of which are completely enjoyable and some of which require more brain and more discipline. Basically, whenever you are at risk of returning to old, useless, self-sabotaging rumination ensure you immediately focus your attention 100% onto a constructive activity or task.

Focusing on constructive activities is the main means of achieving Step Three, where immediately after slipping the self-sabotaging mentation off to the side into your periphery, you instantly shift your focused attention fully onto a brain-demanding constructive activity and keep your attention completely focused on that task. That means concentrating pretty hard on the constructive activity, and as close to 100% as you can get. Where you only focus half-heartedly on a constructive task it is easy to inadvertently allow your attention to drift back onto rumination about old, self-sabotaging themes.

If you have spent many years ruminating on unproductive themes you have built many synapses and neural pathways to physically support an *easy* return to these undesired themes. So, at least initially, it will help you, if you choose constructive tasks that are more brain-demanding and require a fair bit of mental focus to achieve.

For example, it is more brain-demanding to watch a complex TV documentary or a TV show with a complex plot, than to watch a fairly mindless advertising channel on TV. Try to follow the complex plot or documentary, step by logical step and keep your attention as close to 100% on the content as you can. If your focussed attention on the constructive activity is only 85% that means there is 15% of your focused attention available for returning to useless, self-sabotaging rumination themes.

Similarly, it is more brain-demanding to go for a jog or run rather than a walk because it requires much more energy to jog or run so it is almost impossible to ruminate while running whereas it is quite easy to ruminate while walking (unless it is very brisk walking).

If you are not that fit and cannot run or jog long distances when you start, you can probably get around this problem by doing intervals of walking interspersed with short spurts of jogging or running as this will usually keep your body under enough physical pressure that rumination is put on the back burner. But you could equally do some mental mathematics, or make up a rhyming poem, or read a complex book, or do a difficult work task, or play a musical instrument (take up lessons if you would like to but cannot play) or immerse yourself in a vigorous conversation as these activities all use a lot of brain.

One way I like to think about constructive activities is by dividing the 'self' into six different segments and making sure that a little bit of progressive action is taken regularly in all the segments so that no segment gets left too far behind. This is what I meant when I said near the end of Chapter Six about always trying to keep our pieces of 'self' moving forwards in life, to prevent them getting stuck and leading to shutting down. Moving forwards and staying dynamic through tiny incremental progressions helps keep us mentally and physically healthy.

In the next sections I will give you many possible constructive tasks you can choose from. Often constructive activities and tasks done within one segment will overlap with other segments because these activities are very often good for several aspects of self at once. Of course, there are many ways of describing the 'self' but this is one way that I find quite useful.

1. A PERSON'S CAREER

This segment of self is one of the central ways that we obtain meaning and connection with the world. This often occurs through our paid work but it could equally be voluntary work or study. It is the main pursuit people undertake for contributing to a better society.

Nearly all (if not all) work tasks undertaken in our careers, voluntary work or study are constructive activities, and some might include: learning base-line skills, communicating effectively with customers or stakeholders, planning and designing schedules, checking and writing emails, productive meetings with work colleagues, reading work-related material, writing proposals, designing projects, tax and accounting tasks, working on business plans, doing research, applying methodology, administration tasks, improving practical skills, updating social media for business, preparation for public speaking, learning computer programs for work, planning your vision and setting goals, attending seminars, updating skills, negotiating outcomes, thinking, planning and talking about ways to move forward in your career and so on.

2. A PERSON'S PHYSICAL SELF

This part of self-concerns the constructive activities we do to maintain and enhance our physical well-being. It will include researching healthy and nutritious foods to eat and recipes to cook and planning fitness regimes that include attention to cardiovascular health as well as to strength and flexibility and injury prevention.

It will include working out regimes that maximise good sleeping habits so your body and brain can easily rejuvenate. It will later include evaluation of these interventions to see how successful they have been and how they could be improved. Planning and design are in themselves constructive tasks, but once the planning and design are over, then implementation and evaluation become the constructive activities.

Enhancing your physical self can be anything you rationally decide is useful for your health and longevity and may include regular: jogging, swimming, bike-riding, brisk walking, interval training, push-ups, sit-ups, back-strengthening exercises, pull-ups, weights, skipping, yoga, pilates, table-tennis, volleyball, tennis, rock-climbing, basketball, golf, water aerobics, water running, dancing, skating, rollerblading, gardening, tai chi, circuit boxing and flexibility, strength and cardiovascular exercise classes at the local gym.

3. A PERSON'S MENTAL SELF

This segment concerns the many constructive things we can do to enhance the mental self. For example, we can focus on being calm and relaxed by doing Body Flops and always staying below 3/10. Alternatively, we can do mental puzzles that both relax us and enhance our mental flexibility, such as cross-words, Sudoku, word games, making up rhyming poems, mental mathematics (like counting back from 100 by 7's), jigsaws and cryptic puzzles. We can read newspapers, listen to the radio, research subjects on the Internet, read informative magazines, read non-fiction books to increase our general knowledge, and we can read novels to increase our imagination, inner world and emotional intelligence. Some people may engage in spiritual or religious pursuits and others in ethical or social causes.

4. A PERSON'S MAIN HOBBIES AND INTERESTS

This segment addresses many of the constructive pursuits that give us sheer joy and inspire us creatively, helping to provide more meaning in the world. It is good to always have at least two of these going at any one time. Our hobbies and interests often change and need to be fluid as we can easily become enthused while we are caught up in the learning of a new hobby.

Once we are very proficient at a hobby it becomes a useful means of helping us to maintain good self-esteem and a solid sense of who we are.

Although people often think of self-esteem as a vague concept (as though some people are born with it and others are not) it is actually very much tied to how skilled we are at various pursuits in life and therefore how confident we are in implementing them in practice.

It is our ability to be competent and *instrumental* in the world (by being able to act on something and influence outcomes) that is strongly related to how good we feel about ourselves. For example, we can feel good about ourselves when we take up leather craft and work on a piece of leather and turn it into a pair of shoes (a useful outcome) or when we engage in more social interaction and act on a conversation and resolve a conflict (another useful outcome). Hobbies and interests also keep us open to new ideas and frequently put us in contact with other people with whom we can easily relate since we have an easy entry into conversation by sharing the same interest.

Often hobbies and interests overlap with physical pursuits, like rock-climbing, skiing, bush-walking, camping, horse-riding, canoeing, martial arts, sailing, or dancing but they frequently include a huge variety of pursuits like playing musical instruments, craft, knitting, sewing, pattern design, making models of boats/planes, painting, drawing, writing poetry, computer programming, mechanical tinkering, public speaking and debating, computer games, breeding dogs, cats, birds, sheep or roses, collecting stamps, coins, antiques, or jewellery, visiting art galleries or museums, woodwork, DIY projects, pottery classes, assertion classes, animal training, tree-pruning classes, bike-maintenance courses, sculpture, wine making, chess, parenting classes, learning anatomy, first-aid courses, bread-making and cooking classes and so on.

If you don't have many hobbies or interests then think about what you would really love to pursue *if only you had the time*. Then make the time, especially as you will be doing absolutely no ruminating on useless, self-sabotaging thoughts from now on – so that ought to free up a significant amount of time!

5. A PERSON'S INTIMATE AND VERY CLOSE RELATIONSHIPS

This segment involves the constructive things we can do to facilitate the improvement of very close and intimate relationships. You might be surprised to hear that improving intimate and very close relationships is often about developing the constructive skills to help us resolve conflict. This is because, as we go deeper in any relationship and often live in closer quarters, we come across more areas of difference which have to be resolved, if we are to remain close.

There are important skills in assertion that need to be developed by attending courses or therapy or by reading books to ensure that arguments are always calm, outcome focused, stay on track, are friendly, non-blaming and without hidden 'barbs', open-minded, completely transparent, fair, problem-solving (outcome focussed) and rational.

Even though some deeper differences may be argued in an intense manner at times, it is important that there is **never** any loss of control and that each party takes responsibility for ensuring win-win outcomes rather than lose-lose outcomes or stalemates (which will ultimately lead to alienation, bitterness and resentment).

All this takes time, care, proper maintenance and the development of excellent assertion skills. Assertive argument is **always** a constructive activity. On the other hand, sulking, sweeping issues under the carpet, whinging, going silent and stewing or becoming aggressive, abusive or violent are *destructive* and they are behaviours that are best removed from the repertoire. Please see my *Smart Therapy Assertion* booklet for more detail.

As well as constructive resolution through assertive argument, intimate and very close relationships also flourish with some shared constructive interests and projects that are outward focused (like going on outings together like picnics, concerts, sports events and shows), helping each other out with gardening or indoor/outdoor projects like building a shed or painting a room.

To help strengthen intimate relationships it is good to spend regular time alone together without the kids (like going out to the movies or dinner) and ensure you do plenty of general run-of-the-mill talking and sharing about your day with each other to stay connected (especially during the working week when it is easy to become alienated).

Acts of kindness are other constructive activities that help with building goodwill in intimate and very close relationships. They can be small gestures like doing a job for the person when you know they are especially busy at work (like putting the bins out or pumping up their bike tyres) or giving them a shoulder, neck or head rub when they look depleted and worn out or buying them a small gift because you happen to come across it and realise that it is *just what they need*.

These acts show that you love the person and that you are thinking of them, which helps people feel cared for and nurtured, which encourages them to feel more committed to the kindness and safety of the relationship – giving you both a win-win.

6. A PERSON'S WIDER SOCIAL CONTEXT/NETWORK

This part of self is about how to constructively facilitate our connection to wider society and social networks. We know from network analysis research that the more people are connected (even loosely) to wider networks, the more opportunities and choices of progression are available to them. Some people are hugely connected and others are barely connected at all.

Constructive activities are all about progressing us forward, so the more we are widely connected the better. Sometimes this happens fairly automatically when people move upwards in the hierarchy in their career and their business networks grow as they have to consult more widely on big organisational decisions. For other people, who perhaps work in a more solitary fashion (like artists or writers) they have to consciously create wider social networks.

If this does not happen automatically for you through your work then joining clubs is an excellent way to achieve wider social networks. There are clubs everywhere (look online) for whatever you happen to be interested in. There are book clubs, movie clubs, sporting clubs, chess clubs, dining-out clubs, gardening clubs, cooking clubs or knitting clubs. There are groups for learning languages, dog-training, debating, political or social causes.

You could take up scrabble online, comment and participate in social media, or play any number of computer games online with other like-minded people. You could volunteer at an organisation that you support or you could just regularly go out to dinner with friends and acquaintances. But whatever you do, stay connected.

The overall important point here in Step Four, is that whenever you are at risk of starting to ruminate on old, useless, self-sabotaging themes that you would prefer and intend to be free from, then you simply choose a constructive activity from any of the above categories, that fits with your current situation. You might even make a list of your favourite constructive activities that you carry with you in your pocket or wallet for quick reference when the urge to ruminate is intense.

Remember to choose a more brain-demanding constructive activity when the urge to ruminate is strong. For example, doing mental mathematics, or making up a rhyming poem, or listening to talk-back radio if you happen to be in the car, or watching a TV documentary, going for a jog, or reading a complex book if you are at home, or doing a work task, or engaging in vigorous conversation if you are in a work or social context.

As you stop paying attention over time and allow synapses containing old, useless, self-sabotaging material to degrade and break apart, the urge to self-sabotage weakens, and then you can easily choose from a wider number of very relaxing and enjoyable constructive activities that more evenly progress all six segments of your sense of self.

HOW DO I APPLY THE ST STEPS IN PRACTICE?

I want to give you an example of how you can apply the four ST steps in real life. I will describe the detail of a difficult situation and then I'll explain how to use the steps to intervene properly according to ST so that the problem becomes less and less over time rather than bigger and bigger over time.

Let's say that you are engaged in a conversation with a work colleague and suddenly you feel an unpleasant sensation of heat rising to your face and that sensation is almost immediately accompanied by the thought of 'OMG! I'm going to blush and my colleague will think I'm an idiot'. At this stage you have not yet heard of ST, so you pay attention to that thought and then quickly that thought leads to the retrieval of a memory and probably even a visual image that produces more mental exploration and rumination along the lines of 'this happened a few weeks ago when I talked to another colleague and it was so embarrassing and so humiliating'.

You can see that the original heat sensation and scary thought of 'OMG! I'm going to blush and my colleague will think I'm an idiot' has now been compounded by additional focused attention on a memory, making it more likely that you will continue to pay attention and try to make sense of it. Other related synapses from past learning and their mentations are recruited and similarly activated. With all this activation it would be surprising if you did not then experience other thoughts like 'OMG! There is something really wrong with me', as well as some overwhelming feelings of 'humiliation' and 'shame' about both the current and past (memory) situations.

This would then be expected to escalate into an immediate face sweat on top of the original heat, increased heart rate and breathing followed by more and more 'panic' sensations and then other mentations on top. This all happens quickly, usually within a few seconds. This scenario might then result in cutting the conversation short, rushing back to your desk, ruminating and hiding and most likely put you off pursuing future collegial conversations.

In contradistinction, the ST intervention would be that you *keep* having the conversation (Step One) because conversations with work colleagues are usually beneficial and constructive since they provide information that enables you to be effective and progress in your work life (so they are not self-sabotaging) and other people (without the heat sensation) engage in work conversations freely as a normal part of their career.

From the immediate outset in the stress situation, the steps are done so quickly that they are almost jumbled up and simultaneous, where you immediately soften the brain and body into the Body Flop (Step Two) and straight-away (still, at the point of the heat rising to the face) slip the sensation and any thoughts, feelings, images or memories associated with it, off and out of your direct line of focused attention and into your periphery (Step Three).

As you slip these mentations off into your periphery you will probably know what the content of the thoughts are likely to be, but **it is essential** that you do **not** enquire any further about the content and instead you simply slip them all off and away from your focused attention while they are still half-formed (at the first OM ... point). Ensure you not only slide off all the half-formed thoughts, but also **all** other associated mentations including, sensations (of heat or sweats), feelings (of panic or shame), images or memories (of past events) also while they are still half-formed (Step Three continued).

The millisecond that these mentations are slipped off to the side, you engage straight-away in a brain-demanding constructive activity (Step Four), and in this case that would be becoming highly engaged in the work conversation with your colleague. This would be achieved by asking more questions and especially by contributing more input yourself into the conversation, thereby ensuring the conversation becomes more vigorous and demands 100% of your focussed attention.

As part of Step Four, pull your focus away from the strong urge to focus internally (on your shame or embarrassment) and drag your attentional focus (kicking and screaming) onto the external focus of the conversation with your work colleague. Keep your focus there and behave as though absolutely nothing out of the ordinary has happened!

Your conversation is not cut short and if anything, it is extended slightly by your more vigorous contribution. When you eventually do go back to your desk, it is not to ruminate or hide. Instead, you keep your steps in play (always, all the time, every day), and therefore you do not allow yourself to have even a single, self-sabotaging thought about the incident once it has passed. For the rest of the day, you stay immersed in your constructive work tasks. When you go home later, you do not talk to either yourself or anyone else about the incident. Instead you allow it to die a natural death!

PART THREE

HOW DO I USE SMART THERAPY IN PRACTICE?

CHAPTER EIGHT

GERALDINE'S STORY: STRAIGHT-FORWARD ANXIETY

PREAMBLE

There has been a lot of fuss made for decades about all the so-called different types of anxiety, as though they were different entities and required different interventions. On the other hand, I have run a centre devoted to anxiety treatment for more than twenty years and seen thousands of anxious people over that time and, it seems to me that when it is all said and done anxious people just have different 'themes' that scare them, that they then become overly focussed upon.

As I have mentioned, some people are scared of spiders, others are scared of being trapped or scared of flying or of being in the social spotlight or of germs or of the feelings they experience when they panic. Others are scared of their own thoughts, of perhaps having a serious disease or of losing mental control and going mad. Others may fear driving alone (in case they harm others or get stuck in traffic and have to deal with their own feelings and thoughts) and still others fear inadvertently being a murderer, child-molester, being gay or deep down being the 'other' gender. Others fear and ruminate on near-death experiences from the past and others just worry endlessly about pretty much anything, big or small.

What terrifies one person barely bothers another. As I have said, this is to be expected, because we all build our brains in different contexts, and what troubles us is usually specific to what our brains have already identified as 'threatening' in the past. In my experience, intervening the ST way gets rid of them all – so I suggest you don't stress about what 'diagnostic category' your anxiety fits into.

In this chapter and the next chapter, I plan to give some overviews of how anxiety and more complex issues can be treated with ST. In this chapter the story of Geraldine is one that is straight-forward and common, something that I see with slight variations in my work almost every day. After I outline the story, I will then outline the ST steps and interventions that would be applied to the anxiety in order to help fix it. You can use these steps and interventions as templates for how you might get over your own anxiety (no matter what the fear theme).

After reading these stories, you will get the general idea about how to proceed, particularly as ST is simple to apply in practice. Obviously, I cannot cover every contingency but in Chapter Nine I will bring other more complex problems into the mix so you get to see that different issues are also dealt with simply, clearly and logically using ST.

GERALDINE

To begin with let's picture Geraldine. She comes from a background where her father was violent and highly critical and her mother put up with it and tried to 'keep the peace'. Now in her late forties, Geraldine describes how her anxiety started. About ten years ago, Geraldine was out shopping in the city in her work lunch hour, when she suddenly became dizzy, weak in the legs and felt like she might collapse. The incident upset and frightened her making her heart race and causing her to become breathless. She felt sure she must be having a heart attack or stroke. In any case, Geraldine was sure there was something *seriously* wrong with her as she had never experienced these sorts of feelings 'out of the blue' like this before. In the moment it happened she was sure she was dying.

At the time, Geraldine caught a taxi (and rang work to inform them) and was taken straight to an inner-city hospital where they ran a few tests (all of which were clear). The hospital thought there was nothing to be concerned about and she was sent home.

Geraldine tried to push on and went back to work, but she was very worried about what had happened and what might have caused the feeling of 'collapse' and, she was mentally scanning and monitoring her body frequently to see whether there were any signs of it happening again.

Within a few days, Geraldine was having many more 'collapse' feelings and she was full of dread about their occurrence. Geraldine was so worried, she went to her GP for another opinion as she thought the hospital must have missed something. In an attempt to assist her, the GP diagnosed her with an anxiety 'disorder' and, because Geraldine was asking whether there were any types of medication to make it go away, her GP put her on a drug called Xanax.

Soon afterwards, Geraldine started to take time off work because she thought going to work was making her unduly stressed. She hoped that with some days off work she would be able to recover and get back to her old self. Her managing director was sympathetic to begin with but over time and with more days off, he became less so.

Things limped along for a few months but then Geraldine quit work altogether because she thought it was just too much for her and she thought it was making her 'collapse symptoms' worse. She also felt uncomfortable and embarrassed that her work colleagues were frowning at the number of days she was taking off.

Up until quitting, Geraldine had worked in a highly responsible and sought-after role in an organisation with many people under her. She had barely ever missed a day and her career had been very successful and she had valued it enormously, particularly as she was the only one of her siblings to hold down such a responsible role and earn such good money.

But she felt she just had to quit. Now that Geraldine was mostly at home she had plenty of time to ruminate endlessly on her problems. She was able to pay lots of attention to any little change in her internal state: noticing her heart rate, whether she was slightly dizzy, what made her breathless. She noted that 'activity' led to these sensations so she tried to do as little activity as she could. Geraldine gave up running and her gym classes and stopped playing tennis. She no longer even walked fast.

The more Geraldine worried about herself the more Xanax she took to try and alleviate her stress. She also started to notice that contact with many of her friends increased her pulse (which she was taking many times a day now), so she thought they must also be 'stressing her out', so she saw them less and less.

By this time Geraldine was thinking about the risks of collapsing and how to avoid them for many hours every day. When she went out she carried water to keep herself cool, so that it might 'calm' her and she stopped doing anything that might make her slightly more stressed, like going in lifts or catching public transport and after a while she hardly drove at all, and the few times she did drive it was only in her local area. Geraldine had come to feel that longer distances might 'stress her too much' and in any case, she thought she ought to be close to home and hospitals in case anything 'bad' happened.

She often asked her husband to drive her places and even her elderly mother. They mostly wanted to help Geraldine so they did as she asked whenever they could. Gradually, Geraldine stopped driving altogether since she had started to imagine and picture herself so stressed by driving that she would crash into other cars or pedestrians or imagined herself stuck in traffic with that terrible 'collapse feeling' and not being able to escape and stop it.

Even without driving, Geraldine noticed that her heart rate still went up even when she just walked to the local shops. Sometimes in the supermarket she got the 'collapse' sensations and had to take extra Xanax. She made sure she carried them in her bag. She often left the supermarket in a state of sheer panic without buying anything because she could feel the dreaded sensations and feelings coming on. At those times she had thought after thought anticipating what she would do if the collapse feelings became any more intense. She would note all the exits, just in case she 'had to get out fast' and she would not go down any crowded aisles in case she 'got stuck' and could not escape quickly.

Every day felt like a nightmare. Would today be the day she would collapse and faint or have a heart attack? Geraldine worried about it incessantly. She often pulled up old memories and recalled times when she felt faint and told herself how 'awful' it had felt. It seemed hard now to ever have a thought about anything else, and she could barely remember what it felt like not to have to worry all day, every day. She often fantasised about if only she could go back to how she was before the original collapse incident – how 'carefree' she was then before all this started.

THE ST RESPONSE

Even though there is quite a bit here in the case of Geraldine, treating this problem with ST is quite straight-forward. First of all, to elicit the stressful life event that started Geraldine's difficulties, I would hear her story in full and ask her about what was happening in her life not long before her first incident of 'collapse'.

At first, Geraldine would probably struggle to remember and tell me that 'nothing' had happened. This is because Geraldine's anxiety would have become so pronounced and forward-most in her mind that it would have very effectively deflected her attention away from the significance and sadness that was part of her stressful life event.

After a while though, and with some consistent probing, Geraldine would eventually remember that she had met with her boss at work and he was harshly critical of the approach she took on one of the projects she was managing, leading her to feel upset and ashamed about it afterwards. She hated to fail people and often found it devastating to hear criticism. Then, to make matters worse, about a week later there was talk at her work of down-sizing and redundancies and she felt pretty stressed about this, especially in light of her previous conversation with her boss.

Once her 'collapse' feeling happened though, Geraldine had forgotten all about what had occurred at work and believed her 'collapse' experience had just come 'out of the blue'. The two experiences did not appear at all connected, especially as mentations of her imminent 'collapse' felt **so much** more urgent and distressing (since she might literally die at any moment), making the work issues seem insignificant and even trivial by comparison.

Yet if you think about Geraldine's background and how she had built her particular brain, you can see how harsh criticism and possibly losing her job would be an enormous stressor for her. This is because her violent father often criticised her harshly, ridiculing her and sometimes hitting her for good measure. Her mother was weak and provided no advocacy for Geraldine.

Therefore, as a child Geraldine had been deep in a hole, powerless to escape her hard and aggressive father until she grew up. As an adult she had managed to drag herself out of that deep hole, bit by bit, year after year, and she did this largely by working hard at her career, getting many skills and gaining power by earning respect from her colleagues and a decent income for her efforts. Good experiences, skill development and rewards in her career provided Geraldine's self-identity with lots of robust, external validation somewhat counteracting the constant criticism of her father.

Suddenly that could all be taken away from her. Of course, she is stressed! Her fear 'theme' is not even surprising. Her fear is essentially one of 'collapsing' and 'being unable to escape'. In other words, maybe she will fall back into the same deep hole she was in as a child, becoming powerless again, just like her other siblings who had not yet managed to escape the deep hole of their childhood.

You may also notice that Geraldine's fear theme, like so many other themes, has an element of 'not trusting herself' (to remain upright and not collapse). Geraldine no longer trusts herself to be able to deal spontaneously with challenges in life and thinks she must anticipate and plan for all possible contingencies and catastrophes (like getting stuck in a crowded supermarket isle and being unable to escape).

This failure to trust in self frequently comes from difficult childhoods where children have their trust in their own ability systematically undermined. It frequently arises from a background of constant undermining and criticism which makes children learn that there must be something dreadfully defective (and often shameful) about them to warrant all the criticism (and that 'defective' structure could just 'collapse' at any moment).

(In contrast and perhaps surprisingly, learning not to trust yourself can also arise from *parental over-protection* where children learn they have to be protected, from an imaginary dangerous world, because, the implication is that they lack the capacity to look after and defend themselves. This teaches them they cannot trust themselves. This style of parenting is rampant at the moment with children monitored constantly by adults and chaperoned from activity to activity. Unfortunately, I see the results of this in my centre when, later on, the adolescent child or young adult presents with copious anxiety and self-doubt.)

At this point in ST, having heard Geraldine's story I would give her feedback. I would explain the connection between her difficult background and her 'fear theme'. But I would primarily explain to Geraldine the effects of stressful life events and the increases in CRF-induced brain agitation they cause, that then give rise to threatening mentations (like legs going weak, feeling faint or dizzy, pulse racing or thinking she was dying). I would talk about how Geraldine's limbic system was mistaken from the outset – it treated criticism and potential job loss (a metaphor for threat) as an actual life-threatening event, which it was not.

After explaining all this, I would teach Geraldine the four ST steps and teach her how to apply them in her life. In this case **Step One** would be to list all of her problematic behaviours related to her fears of 'collapse' since they are self-sabotaging, fail to be useful or beneficial for her, and because they are not how other people would behave who did not experience anxiety.

Geraldine would need to be brave and start behaving **exactly** like someone who did not have even a shred of anxiety. Although this might sound tricky to her at first, both she and I would know that she can absolutely do it! It doesn't matter how scared she might feel on the inside, she can put one foot in front of the other and insist to herself on keeping going. I would have explained to Geraldine that we all have this capacity because humans (unlike other animals) have a frontal cortex that is able to be *in control* **whenever** we insist on it.

I would encourage her to stop all (or nearly all) of her problematic behaviours in one go if she is up for it. Many people find it is actually easier to change all or most of their problematic behaviours in one go rather than setting up a hierarchy of priority.

Hierarchies can be useful and instil some confidence, where people score out of 100 how 'scary' they find certain normal behaviours and then start with the easiest ones and work through to the harder ones. For example, getting in a lift might be scored by Geraldine at 90/100, whereas walking to the local shops might be scored as 60/100, whereas getting on a tram might be scored as 75/100.

If Geraldine was using a hierarchy, she could first walk regularly to the local shops because it is her lowest score, then catch several trams because it is her next lowest score and then regularly get in lifts because she has worked her way up to her highest score. By this time, Geraldine will have increased her skills and confidence by doing the easier challenges so that her original score of 90/100 for lifts would have reduced to about 70/100 by the time she actually started doing it.

While this all sounds great in theory, it is actually very easy to derail from this method further down the track. That is why I generally encourage people to stop all their relevant self-sabotaging fear-related behaviours at once instead of using a hierarchy. There are a couple of major problems with the hierarchy method. Firstly, hierarchies can be very easily sabotaged, with people going too slowly and losing track. We only have one brain, and it is easy to inadvertently slip back to the old default, self-sabotaging setting. With hierarchies, people often knock out some problem-behaviours (like avoiding trams) only to replace them soon afterwards with other *new* problem-behaviours (like avoiding the phone).

The second reason I slightly discourage the hierarchy method is because I have found in my work that when people want to use it, it often reflects they are less motivated and committed to seriously changing and confronting their problematic behaviours. This makes it less likely to work. Decisiveness and motivation to change are key elements of ST.

I find these less committed people do better with more initial persuasion and theoretical explanation as often they have just missed an elaboration of a crucially important point (usually because I have either forgotten to mention it or I have failed to fully explain the detail due to time constraints), that would otherwise enable them to commit more strongly to change.

In this instance, rather than go to the hierarchy method, I instead go back over explanations to try and find the missing piece of essential information. As the reader of this book, if you found yourself in a similar position, you could go back and re-read sections as a means of increasing your motivation to commence the process with gusto!

This does not mean you must not use the hierarchy method. It just means be very careful of these pitfalls if you do. Make sure you stay on track and move very quickly (within a few weeks) through the hierarchy and that you are highly motivated and can *stay* highly motivated to change throughout this period. On the other hand, if you stop all problematic behaviours at once while you are *extremely* highly motivated my experience is you are also *extremely* likely to succeed.

This does not mean that **every**, single problematic behaviour must be stopped at once – just the relevant ones. With regards to Geraldine, all of her anxiety-related behaviours would be best stopped at once or as close to as possible (within a few days), like not driving, fleeing the supermarket, spending hours every day worrying about collapsing, taking her pulse excessively, stopping physical exertion, not going to work and so on. On the other hand, if Geraldine had smoked for the past 25 years that habit could be noted and a time set to stop it, but it could be postponed for months or perhaps a year (until the essential stuff was dealt with) since it is not directly relevant to the current fear theme. Keep in mind though, that even things which cannot be fixed in a few days (like getting back her job) can be corrected and converted to *constructive* activities by spending that time applying for jobs, re-contacting her old colleagues for leads and fixing her resume.

In practice, all of this means that for Geraldine to do Step One successfully she must go back to tennis, running and her gym classes. She must get back to her old work as soon as possible (preferably, if they will have her back) or find another equivalent job. If she cannot find an equivalent job she ought to take **any** job until she can find a more suitable one. There are consequences of just quitting a job and as a result, Geraldine may have to work her way up again from a lower role – but at least she will be back working again and she will be on an upward trajectory since she has worked her way up before and has the skills to work her way up again, only much quicker this time.

Even though Geraldine did make an error in quitting her job when she became anxious it is important to remember that we all make mistakes and although there are consequences, the most important thing is to correct the mistake as soon as you become aware that you have made it. Geraldine should not waste time ruminating about her mistake, but instead focus on how she can best turn the mistake around and get a good outcome at this point.

In addition for Step One, Geraldine needs to stop carrying water or Xanax (to calm her), get back to driving, drive long distances, and stop asking her husband and elderly mother to drive her places. By this time, her husband and elderly mother will have incorporated driving Geraldine places into *their* sense of self (a good deed which makes them feel good about themselves) so Geraldine will need to learn to very politely and kindly refuse their offers of assistance. Geraldine must also stop talking to her husband and mother (and herself) about her anxiety and when they ask her about it she should say she is 'going well' and leave it at that. Also, Geraldine will have to go to the supermarket frequently and spontaneously, not check for exits, and never flee from the supermarket (**ever again!**).

If Geraldine wants to get over her difficulties then she must also go into lifts, catch public transport, and see her friends regularly again (or make new ones if necessary by joining clubs or similar). Geraldine must be able to walk fast (when appropriate) without inhibiting her pace in case of 'collapse'; stop taking her pulse; and see a GP and get on a titration program to slowly reduce her Xanax – since she is no longer going to need it!

In fact, I would explain to Geraldine that drugs like Xanax actually make anxiety worse in both the longer term and even the shorter term since they are so short-acting that withdrawal symptoms (which are barely distinguishable from anxiety 'symptoms') start soon after ingestion. As such, these short-acting medications are almost constantly creating withdrawal. These anxious and internally agitating withdrawal feelings make people believe their anxiety is exacerbating when really they are just withdrawing from their medication (more on this in Chapter Nine).

If Geraldine were to really put her mind to the task, you would expect that she could reverse all her problematic and self-sabotaging behaviours very quickly indeed, so long as each one was clearly identified with the clear intention of stopping it as soon as possible from a practical perspective. Certainly, Geraldine can take a completely different approach to her life where she simply makes clear decisions about what behaviours she will and will not tolerate in herself right from day one.

Step Two is completed by Geraldine when she restarts her past constructive behaviours which have now become scary due to the development of her fear theme. For example, when she insists on driving long distances again or staying in the supermarket without fleeing or getting in the lift or going back to work, she will be constantly ensuring she is staying below 3/10 in her tension level. This is her job, her responsibility. She has the frontal lobe to do it!

She will never again allow herself to lose control. Every time she reaches 3/10 she will do another Body Flop to take herself lower in her agitation level. On a more analytical level, Geraldine can also do the Getting Real exercise to help her become more objective and realistic about her anxiety. She needs to know that her anxiety 'symptoms' are simply a result of a stressful life event and that she is not going to 'collapse' and that, threatening mentations of 'collapse' are just CRF-fuelled expressions of internal agitation: a simple limbic system error mistaking job threat for life threat. Once she knows this she is able to score her collapse fears in the

Getting Real exercise at more realistic levels like 3/10 compared with truly traumatic events like life imprisonment, death or torture.

Geraldine is also able to enact the Whatever Happens exercise to help calm down her hyper-fuelled limbic system. Geraldine will be literally *begging* the worst to happen, encouraging her most extreme fears, and when she takes off all her brakes and begs for these events to happen, and the dreaded event **still** does not happen – it helps take much of the physiological fuel out of the fear theme.

To do this Geraldine would have to examine what exactly she is terrified would happen if she were to collapse. This examination is done quickly and dispassionately with the constructive frontal lobe, it is **not** an avenue into emotional limbic system rumination.

With quick assessment, we know Geraldine is scared she'll collapse, faint or die (maybe of a stroke or heart attack) and we know she is scared she will not be able to escape the terrifying feelings of collapse.

However, Geraldine has also come from a difficult background where her father was highly critical and violent making her feel 'defective' and in need of his brutal commentary. This led Geraldine not to trust her 'defective' self not to collapse.

With additional probing and self-reflection it becomes obvious to Geraldine that the idea of collapse is partly so scary for her because she is ashamed and embarrassed by her 'hidden defections' that her critical father so readily pointed out to her at every opportunity. In this process of dispassionate examination and self-reflection about what she is really scared of, Geraldine realises that she is worried that if she fainted and collapsed, others coming to her aid may see her defects and imperfections.

Geraldine thinks she has so far managed in her life to hide her deep 'defects' from others, but she is scared that losing control and collapsing will make her unable to hide them any longer. She realises she is scared involuntary things like vomiting, twitching, incontinence or general ugliness (spilling and showing her guts to everyone) might happen if she were to collapse or faint. Consequently, there is also a degree of shame and embarrassment attached to Geraldine's fear.

It is helpful if these elements can also be captured in the Whatever Happens exercise. Once this is done then Geraldine will stand in front of the mirror two or three times a week, or more if she likes, and say the Whatever Happens exercise to herself, out aloud (for increased effect).

Her example would look something like this:

'Whatever happens, happens ... So be it if my intense feelings make me keel over with a stroke in front of everyone today as I walk down the supermarket isle, so be it if I start frothing at the mouth, twitching violently and look completely ugly with everyone standing around me, so be it if I feel so embarrassed by my display that it brings on another massive cardiac event, I'll deal with it, I'll manage, I'll cope. In fact, **bring it on** – Come on, anxiety **go your hardest**, do your worst, **give it everything you've got**! Come on anxiety make me **collapse with a stroke and look completely ridiculous**!'

The Getting Real exercise and the Whatever Happens exercise will help Geraldine in her *long-term* reduction of the physiological fuel underlying her anxiety enabling her to generally stay calm. But in the moment of doing any challenge (like driving or going to the supermarket) Geraldine only needs to do the Body Flop exercise where every time she reaches 3/10 she does the Body Flop to ensure she drops back to 1–2/10.

Then **Step Three** is achieved by never again (outside of the constructive Whatever Happens exercise) allowing herself to have even a single anxious or self-sabotaging thought. Pretty much any sentence that has the words 'collapse', 'stroke', 'heart attack', 'faint', 'failure to escape', 'embarrassment', 'shame', 'vomiting' or 'humiliation' is now off the repertoire. Geraldine will no longer tolerate any 'what if' *thoughts* anticipating catastrophe. Any thought about intense sensations or feelings that she might not be able to cope with are similarly slipped off out of her focused attention and into her periphery. In fact, any thought that is related in any way to her hyped-up anxiety is now off-limits.

Geraldine will also not *picture* herself getting so stressed when driving that she crashes into cars or hits pedestrians and she will not allow herself to *imagine* herself stressed by being unable to escape when stuck in traffic. Geraldine will also not allow herself to mentally scan her body for 'symptoms' of faintness, like weak legs or rapid heart rate. She will, of course, have stopped taking her pulse in Step One. Geraldine will also not allow herself to dredge-up and *recall* old memories of times when she felt faint and how 'awful' that felt.

To achieve all this, Geraldine will remember that she has the same level of control as lifting or stopping lifting her index finger. A mentation is a brain behaviour over which she can exercise 100% control, and it is no different from any other behaviour. The choice is **always** hers to act upon or not and the responsibility **always** stops with Geraldine. Basically, if Geraldine wants to get over her difficulties, then any mentation she wants to reduce cannot be paid focused attention. She will slip all these destructive and self-sabotaging mentations off into her periphery with total disdain and disinterest while they are still half-formed and before they 'stick' in her focussed attention. As soon as she feels these disturbing thoughts rising up from her pre-historic limbic system, Geraldine will wave them off, showing not a shred of interest.

On the other hand, **Step Four** is all about strong focus on constructive activities. Geraldine will be building a highly constructive brain and filling her brain with more and more adaptive, effective and skill-based material. These are the things Geraldine will want to make a larger part of her brain so she can pay attention to them as much as she likes. She will slip off any anxious and self-sabotaging mentations (like dizzy sensations, like worrying she might faint, like her heart racing or thoughts that she might be having a stroke) and instead immediately pay 100% attention to any constructive activity that she has always wanted to do.

For example, if she is driving she might listen and strongly pay attention to talk back radio or she might study food labels in the supermarket to ensure her diet is nutritionally balanced or do some mental mathematics. She can do puzzles and read books while catching public transport and she can *vigorously* engage in conversations with her new or old friends whenever an anxious mentation threatens to emerge, and she can immerse herself in interesting work tasks whenever it suits her – the more of these, the more likely she is to do well in her career again. In short, she will always behave (on the inside and on the outside) **exactly** like a person who has zero anxiety!

On the other hand, Geraldine will **never** flee from the supermarket, or get out of her car to escape, or get out of the lift prematurely by way of 'fleeing' (even if it means going up and down twenty times). While standing in the lift, Geraldine looks completely relaxed, soft and floppy to anyone who is observing her: a completely nonchalant expression. Her face and eyes are calm, relaxed, welcoming and friendly and her body has good posture but it is also relaxed, soft and flexible. Anyone observing Geraldine will think she is a totally calm person. Whenever, Geraldine finishes a challenging task, she is (as always) below 3/10 and has never, in the duration of the task allowed herself to (even slightly) lose control. This is because her prefrontal cortex is *always* the boss no matter how much her limbic system tries to have silly tantrums.

CHAPTER NINE

DANIEL'S STORY: COMPLEX ANXIETY AND OTHER ISSUES

Daniel is a 44-year-old male body builder who works as a security guard. He came from a difficult background where he and his mother were frequently physically assaulted by his alcoholic father who became violent, critical, nasty and unpredictable when he was drunk. Daniel was also beaten up by his much-older brother who was in and out of gaol. Daniel loved his mother but she had few skills and was unable to provide him with much (if any) protection.

Daniel was an anxious child but he tried hard to please his mother and did okay at school, scraping through most subjects and managing (against the odds) to complete high school. Following high school, Daniel joined the armed forces where he did well for many years and enjoyed the opportunities his work provided.

About 4 years after Daniel joined the armed forces he met a bright and 'classy' woman who seemed keen on him. Not long afterwards, they married and had a couple of children. Daniel reported that his wife was a great catch and 'too good for him', saying he couldn't quite believe his luck in marrying her. He was very happy and coping well, even though he sometimes binged on alcohol and acted 'like a bit of smart-arse' when he was drunk. During this period of his life, Daniel stopped all contact with his father and started to really heal.

Then, after nearly 20 years in the armed forces, Daniel was involved in a serious drunken brawl in a pub where he completely lost control and badly injured a couple of men who he believed were behaving obnoxiously towards a woman. As a result, Daniel was subjected to a disciplinary process and forced to resign. He was devastated. The army was all he had known and for the most part he had been very good at his work and had felt stable and contained within it.

Without work, Daniel's mood immediately plummeted, he struggled to sleep, lost his appetite, felt panicky lots of the time, started drinking much more excessively and took up smoking again (after having quit for about 15 years). He suddenly experienced lots of feelings of dread, fear, hostility and anger. He began to fixate strongly on whether his wife loved him and became extremely jealous and angry. Daniel became very insecure about his appearance and started to worry about being ugly, inferior and unattractive, especially to his wife, who he had always felt was 'better' than him and he suddenly felt sure she was going to leave him.

His thoughts felt overwhelming and like they were never-ending: 'what if my marriage breaks up', 'I don't think she loves me anymore', 'I'm ugly', 'I'm disgusting', 'other people are better than me', 'what's wrong with me', 'what if she's repulsed by me', 'how could anyone love me', 'I bet she will leave me', 'I'm sure she'll have an affair'. These fixations were repeated in Daniel's mind over and over, gradually developing into a consistent fear 'theme' that he was *unlovable, ugly, inferior to others, and would be rejected*.

Sometimes, when he had these thoughts, Daniel would become very angry towards his wife, screaming at her and accusing her of not loving him and of having affairs and, although he never hit her, he would slam doors, punch walls, throw and break things. This sudden change in behaviour frightened his wife because Daniel had always been very laid-back and compliant around her in the past.

At around the same time, Daniel started to have 'flashbacks' about his violent father. He would pull up old memories in his mind of getting beaten up, stabbed and kicked as though he was back in the moments when these things had happened. As a child, Daniel had believed his father would kill him and 'it was only a question of *when*' and his images were like a movie playing over and over in his head. When these flashbacks occurred Daniel started to panic, struggling to breathe with his heart racing and his whole body breaking out in a sweat.

Soon after, Daniel started to occasionally have other types of thoughts. He started to think that maybe his wife hated him so much that she might hurt or kill him if he let his guard down. Every now and then he thought he heard her voice whispering to him, saying things like 'you stupid idiot', 'I'll get you, you dirty little bastard', 'your days are numbered, you ugly piece of shit'. There were also times where the voices became louder, like they were shouting at him. When Daniel heard them he would sometimes mutter under his breath, telling the voices to 'shut up' and 'piss off'. Then Daniel noticed his wife was starting to look at him more 'weirdly' (probably with alarm) and he interpreted this as she was 'watching his every move', 'waiting for him to make a mistake' and maybe 'tracking' him.

(Interestingly, with quite a bit of probing, I later found out, to Daniel's surprise, that the 'voices' used the same words and phrases as his father had used to him as a child. He had been so caught up in the emotion of the voices he hadn't noticed. Moreover, upon reflection, Daniel had to admit that those phrases were not consistent with his wife's usual way of talking as she was quite well-spoken. In addition, when I asked him to examine the *exact* quality of the 'voices', he was perplexed and baffled to acknowledge that there was really only *one* voice and the specific quality was very similar to his father's voice even though he was attributing it to his wife!)

Daniel's strange and paranoid behaviour became increasingly frightening to his wife who implored him to get another job and get back to his old self. Daniel, however, was too focussed on his distress to take the necessary action. Then, after a particularly intense altercation his wife got the children dressed, gathered essential possessions, and told Daniel she was leaving, even though he was, by then, crying and literally begging her not to go. Despite his pleading she walked out with the children and their marriage was over.

Daniel felt horribly rejected, which made him feel all the more inferior, ugly and unlovable – playing straight into his fear theme. The worst had happened. Almost as soon as his wife left him, Daniel started to have thoughts flooding into his mind about different ways he might inadvertently kill himself, and these thoughts really terrified him. Although Daniel was miserable, he knew he did not want to die. Yet he kept having thoughts that he might 'accidentally' lose control and step out in front of a bus or train or swerve his car into oncoming traffic.

When he saw the sharp knives in the kitchen he had mental pictures of seeing himself slashing his wrists or stabbing himself or cutting his own throat and seeing blood everywhere. When he saw rope in the garage he visualised hanging himself. Daniel had just developed an additional fear theme, where he was full of *self-doubt and unable to trust himself* to stay alive. He kept hiding the knives (out of his sight), stopped going out to the garage and became excessively cautious on the road.

At this point, Daniel tried to get a grip. His wife had gone and if he was not going to die then he had to somehow help himself. He started to work out at the local gym to get his mind off his increasingly disturbing mentations and to improve his body so he would be more attractive. He got involved in body-building which (although not necessarily ideal) almost certainly saved his life at that time.

The body-building involved high levels of discipline. He had to lift heavy weights over and over, spending hours in the gym with other body builders. He had to eat food 'like it was medicine' eating lots of protein but restricting his intake of carbs or junk food severely so as to lose any excess body fat. He would sometimes 'binge' if he had overly restricted his diet and felt too deprived, but mostly he stuck with it and reduced his fat and became highly 'bulked-up' but lean.

As time went on, he got increasingly involved in the body-building community and attended and entered competitions. Daniel gradually started to do well in the competitions which helped him feel better about himself. He also, however began to check himself too often in the mirror trying to reassure himself, but often finding 'imperfections'. Daniel also became increasingly 'terrified' of fat.

The good thing was that body-building was bit by bit improving his self-esteem, and when he was training hard there was less brain capacity left over for his ruminations about either his wife or inadvertently killing himself, so they eased significantly over time. The voices also gradually reduced in frequency and had, by this time, become more like 'loud thoughts' and were often just single words like 'idiot'.

As he felt better, Daniel became more motivated and was able to find a job as a security guard which fitted in well with his body-building since he looked suitably intimidating. By this time, a couple of years had passed since his wife left him. Around this time, Daniel met and quickly fell in love with a woman body-builder and they started a relationship.

His new partner proved to be very demanding and in-charge. From the outset, she frequently threatened that she would end the relationship if he was not up to scratch. Almost immediately after starting his new relationship, Daniel flipped his fear theme back to his earlier theme of rejection and away from accidentally killing himself. It was just that now instead of being terrified his wife would reject him, he was now terrified his new girlfriend would reject him. At this point, Daniel appeared to lose all interest in his (now) ex-wife and stopped worrying about ways he could accidentally die.

In his new relationship, Daniel was less angry in his behaviours but much more anxious. He spent hours every day worrying about whether or not his girlfriend would finish it. Daniel's behaviour annoyed his new girlfriend and she often rejected his 'needy' requests for affection. Daniel's 'neediness' gave her even more leverage in their relationship than she would have ordinarily claimed, which resulted very quickly in her often withholding her affection and 'dropping' him frequently and then reluctantly taking him back (each time making the conditions more favourable to herself). Her behaviour helped to keep Daniel insecure and chasing her. He was constantly orbiting her, looking for ways to please her and stop her from dropping him.

At this point, Daniel became even more focussed on his body building and increasingly anxious about his appearance. He now spent hours every day checking his muscles in mirrors. He spent nearly all his waking hours worrying about being unlovable, ugly, inferior, and getting rejected by his new girlfriend.

Even though Daniel was rigorously strict with himself during training, driving himself with a punishing routine, he would still occasionally break out and binge on huge amounts of alcohol and/or fatty-foods. His fear of putting on even miniscule amounts of body-fat would then often lead him to purge with vomiting, laxatives, diuretics, or dangerously gruelling gym workouts. He would also often smoke excessively (to try and stop himself eating) in order to get back on track.

It was around this time that Daniel was put on medication (Xanax) by his GP to try and help him calm down. Initially he felt calmer, but very soon he was pill-popping and becoming increasingly anxious and distraught as he was continually withdrawing from his medication. Every time his girlfriend dropped him, Daniel would become stressed out of his brain.

At this stage, Daniel was checking his mobile phone hundreds of times a day to see whether his girlfriend had messaged him. He told her repetitively that he loved her and he bought her excessive gifts (that he could not afford). Daniel even started gambling to try and make money to impress his new girlfriend. Even though Daniel had predominately lost interest in his ex-wife, he still ruminated in an angry way about 'how unfair' it was that she had left him and, (most importantly to him at the time) how his girlfriend was now 'going to do the same', visualising himself all alone and desolate.

Daniel had frequent panic attacks. Since he was very frightened of his panic attacks, he would mentally scan his body for any signs of them and then mentally monitor any signs he found. For example, as soon as he noticed slight increases in his heart rate, sweat-level, nausea or tightness in his breathing he would monitor those physical sensations to see if they got worse. Similarly, as soon as he felt a slight feeling of dread, uneasiness or apprehension he would monitor those feelings to try to gauge whether he was about to have a full-blown panic attack. Though Daniel did not know it at the time, the more he scanned and monitored (paid attention), the more likely he was to induce a full-blown panic attack where he felt totally out of control.

Daniel would also evade all reasonable discussion with his girlfriend whenever she raised issues of (even) minor disagreement between them. Instead of discussing and resolving problems, Daniel would become very passive and compliant with his girlfriend and pretend to agree with her just to 'get her off' his back. Daniel was always trying to increase his contact with his girlfriend and trying to make himself indispensable to her by spending excessive hours doing domestic tasks for her (like cooking her meals, vacuuming, cleaning out her gutters, or cleaning her bathroom), which appeared not to be valued and were certainly not reciprocated.

As time moved on, Daniel's girlfriend was dropping him more and more often. She told him that she could not respect him and that she 'needed space'. He kept chasing and begging her and, from time to time, she would take him back if she needed some help with something. During this time, she would frequently get verbally and physically abusive to Daniel, calling him a 'fucking moron' and a 'useless and pathetic idiot'. On rare occasions, she would also scratch his face, punch and sometimes kick him with frustration. At this stage her physical attacks were ineffectual and half-hearted, but Daniel was concerned they might become more serious.

It was at this point that Daniel came to see me. He was entirely distraught about his situation and wanted me to help him get his girlfriend back (she had just dropped him, yet again). At this stage, Daniel scored his anxiety intensity at 10/10 and he claimed he spent over 10 hours per day on it, mainly worrying and checking his phone repetitively for messages.

Daniel was struggling to hang onto his security guard job because he was so exhausted and so focussed on trying to keep hold of his girlfriend.

THE ST RESPONSE

I noticed immediately that there was a lot to deal with in Daniel, so it was crucial to be systematic.

I heard his story in full and then identified his stressful life events by looking for points where his mentations and behaviours became more exacerbated and extreme, caused by CRF-induced brain agitation. This occurred three times, firstly when Daniel had to leave the army, secondly, when his wife left him and thirdly, when his new girlfriend started threatening to 'drop' him. At each stressful life event, Daniel's fear theme 'morphed' from a fear of rejection (related to his wife) to self-doubt (inadvertently harming himself) and back again to rejection (this time, related to his girlfriend).

Daniel's fear themes were not surprising. During his difficult background, Daniel had been brutally rejected time and time again by his father which meant his brain was already well-practised with the theme of rejection. Once his worse fear eventuated (his wife *actually* left him) then Daniel moved his fear theme onto another well-practised theme from his childhood, namely: self-doubt. His father's endless criticism would have created profound self-doubt in Daniel making it difficult for him to trust himself. (Please see my other book, *Don't Panic* (2004) for a more extended discussion on building brain assumptions.)

I also noticed immediately that Daniel lacked a strong, coherent sense of self. His self-identity was fragile and he easily collapsed under stressful life events. This is likely to occur at a neural level through what is called *cognitive dissonance*, where brain synapses devoted to particular concepts (like self-identity) contain too-much contradictory content. For example, if populations of 'self' synapses are unduly interspersed with negative and undermining content about 'self' it makes it difficult to respond to life challenges as a unified and cohesive synaptic network. This is because positive mentations or actions on behalf of 'self' are immediately met by the disparity of other 'self' synapses whose content contains contradictory information – leading to hesitancy, uncertainty and self-doubt.

This unfortunately happened to Daniel, because much of the empirical evidence around him when he was building his brain and 'self-identity' during his childhood (since his mother was very quiet and passive) was provided by his father constantly criticising him with phrases like he was a 'stupid idiot' or a 'useless piece of shit' which, over time, became *his own internalised explanation* for why he was targeted, beaten and rejected by his father.

It is worth noting that Daniel tries to reduce his cognitive dissonance by excessive mirror gazing (hoping to be reassured and buoyed by his improved body reflecting back at him) but he inevitably finds fault after fault since he has inadvertently learnt and internalised his father's highly-critical gaze, and, therefore all he really notices are his imperfections. So, even though Daniel was trying to reduce cognitive dissonance by mirror-gazing, the strategy becomes self-sabotaging since the outcome sabotages him by leading him to become even more self-critical.

For your information, in my work, I see many self-sabotaging habits that are often established in childhood, where people try to comfort themselves by correcting cognitive dissonance related to their sense of 'self'. For example, behaviours like obsessive skin picking, hair pulling, or nail-biting are attempts to physically scan the body and identify imperfections and then rectify them by removing the imperfect or offensive culprit (the bump on the skin, the stray hair or the rough nail).

The problem is that we can endlessly seek perfection, digging further into the skin, pulling ever more hairs or chewing deeper into the nailbeds. Over time, these habits can also become paired with reinforcing endorphin release when the brain releases natural opiates to lower the pain of self-injury, creating a temporary feeling of calmness that people then continue to seek.

Skin cutting (often with razors) or skin burning (usually with cigarettes) and many other attempts at self-harm including suicide attempts, can also often be seen as ways to rectify cognitive dissonance about 'self' but in the opposite direction. If synapses devoted to negative aspects of self outnumber synapses devoted to positive aspects of self, then the urge might be expected to pull in the direction of self-destruction rather than life affirmation.

In Daniel's case, even though he has many 'self' synapses devoted to internal criticism, he still has enough synapses containing positive content to ensure he wants to live and improve. This would largely result from having had over 20 years in the army (away from his father) and with his (then) loving wife and children; where he would have learnt and incorporated many 'self' skills and positive 'self' experiences into his synaptic content. Against this though, Daniel had still maintained throughout his marriage the notion of being 'defective' and 'inferior' compared with his wife, whom he placed on a pedestal insisting she was 'too good for him'.

When Daniel experienced his stressful life events and allowed himself to get caught in the normal learning cycle, by paying attention for hours every day to his disturbing thoughts (about inferiority and the likelihood of being rejected by his wife), then *related* neural networks were easily activated by synchronous neural firing, giving rise to other threatening mentations, like 'flashbacks' of nearly being killed by his father. In these flashbacks, Daniel is re-living the terrifying moments and activating old childhood and adolescent synapses containing his memories.

These horrific memory retrievals, especially in the context of reduced sleep and excessive CRF, mean that his limbic system, very likely, became so hyper-sensitised and hyper-reactive that it literally 'shouted' at him in the form of voices, rather than communicating via normal, lower intensity, thoughts. At this point, Daniel is so distraught that maybe his limbic system wants to *make sure* it grabs the attention of his frontal (conscious) brain to provide warnings: That if he doesn't stop being '**such a useless piece of shit**', he will '**get killed**!' Daniel simply reassigns the memory of his father's voice to his wife, because that is the current context of his perceived threat.

Although we simply don't yet know for certain, in some forms of psychosis (where people hear voices) there may be an organic or genetic component. On the other hand, what I tend to see in my clinical practice is where CRF has most likely ramped up the intensity or salience of neural transmission to such an extent that the frontal brain in its top-down analysis 'reads' and interprets the much higher intensity of signalling as being most similar to what external voices sound like (i.e. louder). The frontal brain is thereby likely to misattribute overly-intense *internal* signals to an *external* voice. I find in my work with intense anxiety, that where people hear voices these tend to reduce naturally once stress lowers, particularly, when people are taught **not** to pay attention to the voices.

Note that once Daniel starts to help himself and takes up the brain-demanding and constructive activity of body-building and finds himself a job, he is able to reduce his neural network activation by ruminating less and paying less attention; and as a result, the voices become fewer and change their quality from that of 'voices' to occasional loud 'thoughts'.

Another broad aspect I would mull over at this point is that Daniel also has a minor fear theme that he has inadvertently created, almost as a side-line from his body-building due to the intense attentional focus required on the appearance of his body. He becomes very frightened of fat and develops excessive habits of mirror-checking to ensure he is reducing his fat to muscle ratio. Interestingly, this is the common 'fear theme' of people with 'anorexia nervosa' who also frequently develop mirror-checking behaviours to check they are sufficiently skinny.

Like with Daniel, people who develop anorexia often do so as part of an initially constructive and adaptive response to CRF-induced distress. They try to take action to increase control. Daniel took up body-building when things became unsustainable, as a counter to his distress; as a means to improve his self-esteem and increase his control over his own body. This was a very sensible intervention, and it saved his life at that point. Similarly, people with anorexia often experience stressful life events (like parents divorcing) and, feeling out of their depth and powerless to control events around them, they opt to control the one thing that they feel is within their control: their own bodies.

Again, this is a sensible response: It is great to get healthy, lean, fit and strong. But the response needs to be tempered and controlled so that it does not become excessive, which can sometimes happen if there are not enough other avenues developed to increase self-esteem. If we pay attention predominantly to only one focus then that focus can take up more and more of our brain and we can easily become fixated. While it is good to be lean, healthy, fit and strong, it is not good to be terrified of fat, unhealthily thin and unable to have a relaxed attitude to food.

It is best to have more strings to our bows, and to tap into parallel learning cycles for many different competencies so one focus (like appearance) does not become too fixated upon. At this point, a stronger, more robust sense of self is required. We build a stronger sense of self by taking up and applying ourselves to *many* constructive interests that we become increasingly skilled at, thereby over time, building ever more synapses devoted to positive and constructive aspects of 'self' so that cognitive dissonance reduces.

We must *always* control our behaviours, not have our behaviours control us. When people begin purging by vomiting, diuretics, excessive exercise, cigarettes or laxatives they have lost control. Our behaviours always need to remain within the ST parameters of useful, functional, effective and never self-sabotaging. In this situation, we would ask ourselves, how and what would another person eat who was not scared of 'fat' yet was also healthy, fit, lean and strong – we would watch their behaviour (and if possible, ask them about it) and then copy it. We would also take up several other constructive pursuits to develop our self-esteem in other directions to keep the focus more balanced and less appearance-based.

Following Daniel telling his story, my feedback for his self-rescue would take the form of the ST Diagram (page 39) with his specific details incorporated, and it would essentially consist of five parts. Firstly, what had *started* his difficulties: namely, his difficult background ('priming' him to pay attention to threatening mentations); and secondly, his stressful life events, leading to CRF-induced brain agitation and the production of numerous threatening mentations.

Thirdly, Daniel's feedback would consist of what was *maintaining* or keeping his difficulties going: namely, paying attention to these threatening mentations and (inadvertently) building new and strengthening old conceptually-related synapses and thereby making his fears and insecurities a bigger and bigger part of his brain.

Fourthly, we would discuss how paying excessive attention has increased the intensity of his threatening mentations (making them even more frightening), causing Daniel to have strong urges to find 'solutions' even if out of desperation, his 'solutions' were ineffectual, escapist or self-sabotaging. As a result, Daniel took up many behaviours (to try to reduce his fear of rejection) that have subsequently become self-sabotaging over the longer-term, like binge-eating, excessive food restriction, smoking, binge-drinking, excessive phone-checking, mirror-gazing, anger (in the past), compliance (currently), taking sedatives, taking laxatives and diuretics, chasing his girlfriend, and gambling.

I would explain to Daniel that these self-sabotaging 'solutions' teach him (completely incorrectly) that he cannot survive without them. This wrongly teaches Daniel that he has to keep doing them or else he will go under. The more Daniel pays attention to the idea that he 'cannot cope' without employing these desperate 'solutions' the more this (false) idea is drawn into his normal learning cycle, where it is learned, consolidated and retrieved. This keeps Daniel's fear theme of rejection intense, urging him to pay even more attention to it and his ineffectual 'solutions' which also keeps his dendritic spines (devoted to these 'themes') popping up in disproportionate numbers.

For example, the more he chases his girlfriend, uses alcohol or checks his phone to try to dampen his fears of rejection, the less he demonstrates to himself that he can survive (perfectly well) if he is 'dropped' or rejected. This then maintains the intensity of his fear of rejection and keeps him paying attention to any future conceptually-related mentations. To add insult to injury, some of Daniel's self-sabotaging behaviours (like sedatives or alcohol) have physiologically-addictive cycles helping to further keep them in place.

Fifthly, the feedback would consist of exactly what Daniel needs to do to *fix* his difficulties: namely stop paying attention to threatening mentations and convert his self-sabotaging and dysfunctional escape behaviours into constructive pursuits that will serve him well and allow him to progress in his life.

Up until this point, Daniel has been behaving as though he has no control over his mentations or behaviours. He will really need to grasp that he actually has 100% voluntary control over what he allows into his focussed attention and that he can slip any unhelpful or destructive mentations off into his periphery so that they become, very quickly over time, a smaller and smaller part of his brain.

Daniel will have to understand that **every single time** he allows himself to pay attention to his anxiety, anger, rejection, self-doubt, smoking, drinking, physical imperfections and so on, he is markedly increasing the proliferation of dendritic spines that will then create hundreds of thousands of **new** synapses devoted specifically to 'holding' all these bits of information. Any new synapses will materially (at a physical level) support the very 'themes' Daniel wants desperately to obliterate.

Daniel must understand that every time he makes the choice to pay attention to these unwanted themes, he is instructing and directing his perfectly normal brain to learn and lay-down the content to which he is paying attention. His brain will readily cooperate: It will learn anxiety, smoking, physics, binge-drinking, maths, music, anger, computer programing, fear of rejection, self-doubt, gambling, mirror-gazing for imperfections, statistics or a foreign language equally effectively.

Therefore, Daniel must be clear that the way he builds his brain is from now on is entirely *his choice* and *he is responsible* for his own brain content going forward. He was not responsible for how he built his brain as a child, but as an adult the buck stops with him. This means that even though he has a long list of self-sabotaging, escape behaviours they are all 100% under his voluntary mental control and the choice is his as to whether or not he decides to get rid of them or keep them. In the future, it is Daniel who will live with the consequences of his behaviour and he must fully grasp the importance of *always staying in control*.

In accepting he is now the boss of his own brain and responsible for what his brain contains, he must face squarely that many of his difficulties in his adult years have been created by his own behaviours and brain-responses. While this may appear to 'blame the victim' nothing could be further from the truth. Daniel had no knowledge that paying attention would make his fears worse, and he cannot be blamed when he had no intent. In any case, please recall that blame **never** enters the teleological framework, which looks simply at contribution to outcome and how to change that contribution to get a better future outcome.

Most importantly though, it is only when Daniel *learns and understands* his contribution to his problems that he is able to harness the necessary *power* he requires to *stop* his contribution. Where he is contributing to his problems he can remove his contribution; if he were not contributing he could do nothing and would be powerless against his problems. In other words, by owning his contribution, **there is something *he* can do to fix it all up**! The bigger his contribution, the **more** he can do! Understanding the buck stops with him is *exactly* what Daniel must grasp in order to dig deep and galvanise his own **huge resources to save himself**!

While I can assist Daniel (and I will do everything in my power to do so), in the end he will sink or swim under his own steam. Depriving him of taking responsibility for his own contribution would be the single largest mistake as a therapist that I could make, since by doing so I would leave Daniel believing he was a powerless 'victim' who was unable to rescue himself. Once Daniel clearly grasped and understood this information then we would start work on the four ST steps of self-rescue.

Step One involves Daniel ensuring all his behaviours are useful, functional and not self-sabotaging. Since most of Daniel's presentation is about many dysfunctional, out-of-control behaviours, then much of his self-rescue will be spent on correcting these problematic behaviours.

Some behaviours like punching walls, slamming doors, screaming or throwing things out of anger or hiding knives, avoiding going out to the garage, or being excessively cautious on the road, are past behaviours that are related to his old fear theme of not being able to trust himself not to accidentally harm himself. Even being excessively cautious on the road is self-sabotaging as it is likely to lead to excessive hesitation followed by unpredictable last-minute accelerations, manoeuvres, or 'freezes' that are more likely to result in injury. Balanced levels of caution and confidence leading to calm, relaxed, controlled driving-behaviour is preferable.

Even though all of these problematic behaviours *only* occurred in the lead up and immediate aftermath of his marriage breakdown, they still must be written-down and listed as self-sabotaging behaviours as part of Step One, and Daniel needs to acknowledge the importance that he **never** re-engage in them again. This is because, under the stress of future stressful life events when CRF-induced brain agitation becomes high again, past behaviours can sometimes get reactivated and it is important that Daniel knows these maladaptive behaviours are off his repertoire forever and that he has 100% control over this.

It is also important that Daniel understands that his *angry* behaviours were just the flip-side of his current *compliant* behaviours, and that both of them are equally problematic and both will have to go. For more detail on this please see my *Smart Therapy Assertion* booklet. However, in short aggression and compliance behaviours are both driven from a place of *fear of conflict* which Daniel learnt in his childhood from his frightening father. Aggression is a ferocious response to conflict that is usually used when the 'enemy' is perceived as weaker or when it is felt there is *nothing left to lose*. In contrast, compliance is a hiding or 'disappearing under the radar' response to conflict that is usually used when the 'enemy' is perceived as more powerful (can hurt you), and/or where there is little or no chance of escape.

Until now Daniel has been constantly complying and placating his girlfriend by smoothing over the slightest disagreement with him yielding to her will. If Daniel is to have any chance of a meaningful, equal, honest and genuinely loving relationship he needs to discuss differences openly and calmly. Daniel will need to resolve as many issues as possible in order to get on the same page as his girlfriend, so that they have more in common in their perspectives in life and can therefore become more united.

Daniel will have to learn to stop resorting to *either* aggression or compliance going forward in his life generally and in his relationship since they both ultimately shut down fluid communication and prevent effective problem-solving. Instead Daniel will have to learn to be assertive by coming forward to engage in conflict in a kind, friendly, direct, soft but strong manner. He will need to practise talking issues through at length without just caving-in, and over time, this new behaviour will teach Daniel to become more his 'own person', with heightened levels of self-respect.

Daniel also has to teach his brain that he can easily tolerate the risk of losing his girlfriend, and he will do this by deciding to stop his excessive chasing, gift-giving, mobile-phone-checking, job-doing, gambling-to-impress, repetitive-I-love-you behaviours. Instead, while Daniel is learning to rein in his excessive behaviours he will 'mirror' her. This means that if his girlfriend gives him a gift he can reciprocate; if she tells him she loves him then he can tell her; or if his girlfriend openly requests he do a job for her, he can agree and cooperate but only on the basis that he asks her to do one for him (even if he does not really need it done). Once reciprocity is established it can become more relaxed, but initially Daniel needs to break his old habits. Incidentally, to win his girlfriend back after being 'dropped', all Daniel has to do is stop chasing her and his girlfriend immediately regains her interest.

Daniel will also need to change his behaviour relating to his 100 times a day mobile-phone-checking. From now on, apart from when he hears his phone go off, he will reduce checking it to a functional and effective frequency of 4–6 times a day maximum unless there is a genuine emergency. To do more would fail to break his established habit of over-checking. Later, once his over-checking habit was broken and he was relaxed he could increase it slightly, always keeping in mind though that ST behaviours are always functional. Over-checking a phone takes time, and reduces overall behavioural efficiency for other necessary daily tasks.

Another behavioural change Daniel must make is to pull his girlfriend up every single time *before* she starts to use abusive language towards him like 'fucking moron' or 'useless pathetic idiot' and he must certainly never tolerate her scratching, punching or kicking him. By tolerating her abusive behaviour in the past he has effectively taught her that there are no consequences for her appalling behaviour. When there are no consequences people tend to keep exacerbating their behaviour as though in a vacuum as there are no external restraints giving signals of containment. Humans are very socially embedded in our learning, so we are very responsive to external limits.

By this time, his girlfriend has already learned to escalate very quickly as we all become increasingly efficient and 'normalised' in our behaviours the more we practise them, so he will have to correct her at a point where she will probably not even be aware that she is becoming frustrated, since her escalation will feel so 'normal' to her. He will have to correct her *every* time she rolls her eyes, shakes her head, huffs and puffs, hisses, clucks her tongue, gets jerky in her movements, glares at him, or ever so briefly curls her lip, purses her mouth, or mutters through clenched teeth, all in contempt of him. These behaviours typically occur before actual (or more overt) verbal abuse, but they occur for briefer and briefer amounts of time as perpetrators get more practised in efficient escalation, so the window of opportunity for correction is a fairly small one for Daniel by this stage.

Daniel must catch her *the second* he observes her intensifying her agitation and he must *grasp the initiative*, saying in a very calm, measured and authoritative voice (think of a school principal): 'Just stop that will you. I'm not willing to have you behave so contemptuously towards me. Do you realise that you are making a "hissing" sound [or whatever it is that she is doing – be specific]. I think you know that I demonstrate kind and respectful behaviour towards you and I *absolutely* expect the same back in return. While we don't have to agree on issues, we do need to be able to talk about them in a calm and rational manner, so you need to calm down'.

His girlfriend would probably continue to escalate for the first couple of times that Daniel stands up to her, in order to test him out since she has been able to get away with her behaviour in the past. If she does continue to escalate, it is crucial that Daniel *keeps the initiative* and says something like, 'Have you absolutely **no** self-respect? Truly, if you want to behave like a three-year old, go ahead and do it – but do it on your own, in your own *miserable, pathetic* little world – because your anger is so ugly at this moment that no one would ever want to be around you. I'm warning you now that if you don't calm down immediately, then I'm leaving'. Note that there is no pleading with her, no begging, Daniel's voice must be direct, authoritative, calm, measured, projected, soft but strong, and in *total* control.

If his girlfriend remained escalated then he would immediately **stop conversing**, gather his things and leave her on her own (without another word), thereby putting in place a negative consequence. The more of a negative consequence she needed, the longer he would stay away which could be hours, days, weeks, or forever if required. Whatever the case, Daniel needs practice at effectively 'dropping' her.

Should Daniel miss the window of opportunity and his girlfriend has already progressed to behaviours like yelling, screaming, snarling, spitting, barring her teeth, slamming doors, breaking objects, threatening him or actually getting physical with him and really displaying the ugly side of unrestrained aggression, then he must leave immediately and ensure he calls the police, since them *just arriving* is a negative consequence for her as she will have to explain herself and suffer their lack of approval.

Most importantly, the police will very likely impose some of their own more formal and serious negative consequences like admission to a psychiatric unit, overnight lock-up, or laying of assault or criminal damage charges (if she destroys property in her rage) and she will then have the added inconvenience of having to make court appearances, pay fines or do gaol time.

In this case, Daniel is not yet at the point with his girlfriend where she is likely to kill him, but he must never let it get anywhere near this stage. He must leave her permanently (and, cleverly, without trace if necessary) well before it ever reaches the point of her inflicting more serious damage (like choking) or reaching for weapons (like bottles or knives) and certainly, he must leave well before threats of house imprisonment.

Domestic violence is rarely ever like random street violence. It almost always has observable and predictable escalation over time that must be nipped in the bud extremely **early**. Once it reaches the level of weapons and has a more calculated aspect to it like forced imprisonment, it will be a whole different scenario, all bets will be off, and the outcomes will frequently be tragic. So it is essential he sets clear limits early.

Also as part of Step One, Daniel needs to address his poor sleep. To achieve this, he will have to put in place a regular routine where he gets to bed early enough (so he does not become agitated from over-tiredness and is therefore unable to sleep) and where he gets up at the same time irrespective of how much sleep he has had (even if it is no sleep at all). For example, he might decide that he gets into bed at 9.30 pm and gets up at 6 am. Even on the weekends, especially in the early stages of establishing this new habit, he should try not to vary his times by more than about an hour at either end. Even if Daniel barely sleeps in the first few days, he will sleep soon enough so long as he sticks with this new routine.

Daniel will also make his bedroom as dark as possible and ensure he is not too hot and that he is not overstimulated by coffee, caffeinated tea or withdrawing from sedative medications (which lead to high levels of withdrawal agitation often several hours after taking them). To come off his Xanax medication, Daniel needs to visit his GP and ask for a titration program where he gradually reduces the amounts he is taking. This is often a slow process over many months, as fast withdrawal from sedating substances (like alcohol, antipsychotic, sleeping and, some antidepressant medications) is extremely dangerous and can result in death. With Daniel's binge-drinking, since he is not drinking every day he can quit without a titration program.

As part of developing his regular routine, Daniel should try as much as possible to do his hardest and most brain-demanding work earlier in the day, gradually winding down towards bedtime and he should not use any bright screens (TV, tablet, mobile phone) in the last hour before he goes to bed as the bright screen destroys melatonin, which is his main sleep hormone. Instead he could lie on the couch for the last hour and read a book or magazine – which will not overstimulate him, and therefore allow him to notice that he is getting tired.

As soon as he feels sufficiently tired, Daniel should get up and go to bed, and simply enjoy the lovely feeling of rest while just 'emptying his mind'. If he struggles to fall asleep after about half an hour then he can get up and read again on the couch and keep repeating the process as necessary. He should never lie in bed worrying as this will train his brain that going to bed is the place and time where he ruminates and over-thinks issues.

Even though Daniel's sleep problems are fairly severe, if this routine is followed, his brain will learn his new habit extremely fast and the new habit will be established quickly. The hardest part is in the first few days where he will have to get up at a set time, often having had very little sleep. The worst thing he can do is to stay in bed and oversleep as this will retard his sleep pattern further and further in a self-sabotaging direction. It is amazing though, with a solid routine just how quickly his brain will learn and adjust to his new desired habit.

Daniel will also decide to quit smoking, binge-drinking and gambling, since they are all highly destructive habits for his health and financial security. To quit these habits, Daniel will predominantly have to quit *thinking* about them (so more on this in Step Three). For the time being, Daniel will just have to make the firm commitment to himself that he will not carry out any of the actual behaviours of binge-drinking, smoking or gambling.

He ought to decide to quit them all for at least a period of two years, and then re-evaluate how he is going in his life without them at that stage, and then preferably undertake to stay off them all permanently.

After the necessary two years of breaking the neural habit, some people choose to return to controlled levels of their habit if it benefits them socially to do so. For example, *some* people who were previously alcohol-dependent can after two years of not drinking (and the corresponding neural pathway disintegration) manage to drink 'socially' from then onwards, but only if they *strictly* keep themselves to never exceeding two standard alcoholic drinks per week. I have found in my clinic that if people exceed this precise amount, then the neural pathways easily re-form, creating unpleasant and strong urges for them to drink excessively again. Often it is just easier for people to quit forever. To help him do this, Daniel will need to take up other constructive interests and hobbies that he enjoys and which will build his self-esteem to replace his dysfunctional ones (so more on this in Step Four).

Also, as part of Step One, Daniel needs to work out a better routine with his eating so he does not swing from binge-eating and gorging on food to starvation, vomiting, gruelling workouts, diuretics, laxatives and smoking followed by over-eating again because he feels so deprived. To help with this, Daniel needs to bring other constructive activities into his life, so that his self-esteem is not so dependent on his appearance from body-building. Then, over time as other sources of self-esteem become a bigger part of his brain, Daniel can gradually make body-building a smaller and smaller part of his life since it is probably not so healthy for him.

Body-builders frequently put on excessive muscle quickly, without sufficiently developing their cardiovascular systems. This means their small hearts suddenly have to pump and supply blood and oxygen to this enormous muscle bulk, sometimes leading to fatal infarct. In addition, although Daniel denied it, I'm pretty sure he was on anabolic steroids which, even if 'cycled' correctly with proper rest periods, can still have serious side-effects like hypertension, blood clotting, heart attack, stroke, liver and kidney disease, irritability, suicidality, not to mention baldness, testicular shrinkage, infertility and erectile dysfunction.

Daniel needs an emphasis and focus on *genuine* health (not a pseudo-appearance of it by having muscle and barely any body fat). Genuine health requires a well-balanced, highly nutritious diet that is relaxed and easy to manage, combined with a balanced and enjoyable lifestyle that includes moderate exercise that maintains strength, flexibility and a robust cardio-vascular system.

A well-balanced, highly nutritious diet means lots of fresh, 'live' food (for example raw or lightly-cooked vegetables and fruits) and very little processed food, in amounts that are satisfying and do not make Daniel feel deprived (or he will swing into over-eating, gruelling workouts, smoking, laxatives, diuretics or vomiting). It goes without saying that Daniel must decide clearly to stop his use of laxatives and diuretics and cease vomiting (which can upset electrolyte balance and result in heart attack), and he must commit to a definite date to cease smoking to give his body a reasonable chance of recovery so as not to develop health problems like heart and brain infarct, emphysema, limb amputation, and various cancers.

To keep a diet relaxed, people often nowadays apply the 80–20 rule where 80 percent of the time they ensure high-quality nutrition from the main food groups and 20 percent of the time they eat satisfying, but less strictly-healthy food.

Daniel needs to be aware that eating anything more than 20% especially of starchy foods (white rice, bread, pastas, pastry, chips, peeled potatoes) or sweet foods (soft drinks, lollies, cakes or too much fruit) will set off a powerful insulin response that will suddenly force large amounts of glucose into the cells thereby dropping the blood glucose level and creating enormous increases in appetite shortly after large intake.

Huge appetite increases often make people feel *out of control* in their eating (thinking they have a psychological problem with food) when all that is really happening is an excessive insulin response, usually due to overeating starches or sweets. Daniel will do better if he largely tries to flat-line his insulin response, which will also place less strain on his pancreas, making it less prone to failure going forward.

Making the decision to change all these behaviours will be a big shift for Daniel, but one he can easily achieve since they are all 100% under voluntary control. Most of the work Daniel needs to do for his specific self-rescue lies within Step One as his presentation is one of numerous out-of-control behaviours. If he wants, Daniel can make the decision to stop them all *immediately*, apart from his Xanax addiction which must be slowly reduced. This would be the most effective course of action.

Otherwise, if Daniel preferred he could stop his self-sabotaging behaviours systematically over time so long as he always *keeps strict track* of what, when and how his next problematic behaviour will be stopped. If Daniel chooses to take this pathway he must ensure the process occurs as quickly as possible so he maintains his motivation and momentum, and does not replace old dysfunctional habits with new dysfunctional ones. Very soon (within 6 weeks or less of changing these problematic behaviours), Daniel will barely have any urges to do them again and he will develop into a highly-functional and effective person.

Step Two will get Daniel to calm down. Daniel frequently experiences increased heart-rate, sweats, difficulty breathing, feelings of anxiety and dread, and worrying thoughts about having panic attacks that lead him to scan and monitor his body for exacerbation. When he is highly stressed he also pulls up visual images and memories in the form of flashbacks and has such a physiologically hyped-up limbic system that he occasionally hears voices or loud thoughts. For Daniel always staying below 3/10 will help him enormously to stay in control at all times.

To do this, he will need to practice his Body Flop exercise and do it many times per day, being absolutely clear that the buck stops with him. Once Daniel has practised his Body Flop exercise about a dozen times, he will become very efficient at *simultaneously* quietening and dampening the chatter in his brain (duvet image); while releasing every muscle and sinew downwards into a complete state of floppiness and relaxation; and doing a single exhalation of his breath while he releases any inner, emotional tension.

Since the Body Flop only takes a few seconds to do (once practised), it will impact his time very little (less than 4 minutes) even if he does 50 Body Flops per day. It is *his job* to ensure he never again allows himself to get above 3/10 irrespective of what is happening around him. As soon as he reaches 3/10 he must do the Body Flop to drop back down to 1–2/10. If he inadvertently reaches higher levels of stress then he must do several Body Flops until he is back fully in control and below 3/10.

Daniel also scores his anxiety level at 10/10. Although his anxiety feels very intense to Daniel he needs to do the Getting Real exercise, where he assesses other real-life potential events like life imprisonment, confinement in old age, systematic torture, severe chronic pain, or facing his own death. The realistic appraisal of his anxiety needs to be scored as more realistic and mild by comparison. He must stop being excessively catastrophic in his scoring and instead readjust his anxiety score down to a more realistic 3/10.

Daniel can also do the Whatever Happens exercise to help weaken the over-reaction of his limbic system, where he dares and practically 'begs' his worst imagined fear to happen, yet survives it – taking the power and fuel out of his anxiety theme of rejection and allowing him to calm down. For Daniel, his exercise would look something like this:

'Whatever happens, happens ... So be it if Caroline [his girlfriend] dumps me yet again today, so be it if she thinks I am as grotesque and ugly and repulsive as a maggot, so be it if I am left all on my lonesome, excluded by everyone and hated by the masses, I'll deal with it, I'll manage, I'll cope. In fact, **bring it on** – Come on, anxiety **go your hardest**, do your worst, **give it everything you've got**! Come on anxiety make me **feel utterly rejected**!'

Daniel can practise this exercise in front of the mirror, saying the words out aloud to give them reinforcement. He can say the words with glee, defiance and insubordination, caring not remotely for his past fears and cautions.

Daniel will also invoke Step Two and always stay below 3/10 even when he has the most frightening and threatening mentations going forward, and he will often choose to do the Body Flop (as his constructive activity of choice) at exactly those moments.

Step Three will be crucially important for Daniel. He must always know that he has complete 100% control over what mentations he allows into his focussed attention. Any mentations he wants to become a smaller part of his mental experience need to be slipped off, effortlessly, into his periphery and treated with complete disinterest. Daniel can respond to his various mentations with internal comments like 'What a silly thought', or 'Who cares about that ridiculous sensation', or 'I couldn't care less about my idiotic feelings', or 'I'm no longer *even slightly* interested in that memory or image'. He ought to be waving these mentations off into his periphery while they are still half-formed and before they 'stick'. Should Daniel find that he has inadvertently paid attention to an unwanted mentation, then he ought to slip it off as soon as he becomes aware. Once in his periphery, Daniel may know the unwanted mentation is vaguely there, but he also knows he has no intention of bringing it into back into his focussed attention.

Daniel does this with all of his unwanted mentations. He ceases all mental scanning and monitoring. In the past, Daniel has tried to *explore, scan his body and find* any *sensations* of panic, like increased heart-rate, shortness of breath, nausea, or outbreaks of sweat; and he has sought out any *feelings* of anxiety, fear, dread, anger, hostility, powerlessness or jealousy. Now Daniel has to undertake to completely ignore all of these sensations and feelings, as well as ignore any *urges* to smoke, drink, gamble, be compliant, give-excessive gifts, or chase his girlfriend. Similarly, Daniel must slide off any *thoughts* about rejection, self-doubt, inferiority, ugliness, cigarettes, alcohol, gambling, not-coping, compliance, gift-giving, or chasing his girlfriend. Slipped off into the periphery will also be any old, useless, self-sabotaging *memories* or *images* like flashbacks.

With some quick explanation, Daniel can learn to recognise the difference in sound 'quality' between a normal thought and an overly-salient (psychotic) thought that is interpreted (because of its CRF-fuelled intensity) as an external 'voice' or 'loud' thought. The psychotic *voices* have less clarity and have a slightly 'vague' and 'echo' quality to them compared with real voices. The 'loud' *thoughts* have less fluidity than normal thoughts and 'jolt' slightly because they have a slight sound quality to them in a way that normal thoughts do not. Daniel does not need to be afraid of these perceptual misinterpretations and he will treat the 'voices' or 'loud' thoughts with complete disinterest, slipping them off gently into his periphery and paying not a shred of attention to their content.

Daniel will also slide off any *visual images* of blood, wrist or throat-cutting, self-stabbing, hanging himself, or visualising himself all alone and desolate. As part of slipping-off visual images, Daniel must also slide-off any *memories* and flashbacks of his violent childhood and near-death experiences with his father and he will show complete disinterest in all of them, slipping them into his periphery when they are still half-formed and before they 'stick' in his frontal attention.

Daniel must always be clear that the threats from his difficult background simply trained him to nearly always pay attention to the part of his brain where threat is detected and processed, namely, his limbic system. Excessive limbic attention on all those messed-up agitations led him to believe he had no control over them. Daniel needs to understand that this is a complete fallacy. As an adult, with a fully-developed brain Daniel has complete control (100% control) and he can now decide to ignore his limbic system (even when it tries to have a tantrum) and focus predominantly on his frontal, rational and strategic brain. Daniel can now exert the necessary discipline with his frontal brain to stay on course in his life going forward.

Step Three is also highly relevant for Daniel in changing problematic, self-sabotaging behaviours like binge-drinking, smoking or gambling. He needs to note that there are *easy* and *hard* ways to quit problematic behavioural habits. The hard way is slow and gruelling and almost inevitably results in returning to the problematic habit. The easy way is fast, efficient and successful, like flicking a switch if done correctly.

For example, if Daniel decided to quit smoking, the **hard** way would be to quit cold-turkey, without nicotine patches. He would stop buying, botting, and putting cigarettes in his mouth, BUT he would still allow himself to *think* about cigarettes, like 'oh wouldn't a cigarette be lovely now', 'I remember I used to smoke whenever I was on the phone or after a meal', 'smoking used to give me such a sensation of calmness', 'I can just picture myself having one', 'I've given up for 3 weeks now, surely I've proved my point – I know I can quit, so it won't hurt me to have the occasional one', 'I deserve it, I've had a tough day, I really *feel* like one', and 'in any case, surely one won't hurt me'. If Daniel allows himself to keep thinking about cigarettes, or pay attention to any other mentations about them, like sensations, feelings (urges), images, or memories, he will almost certainly start smoking again.

On the other hand, the **easy** way to quit any behavioural habit including smoking is **to stop thinking about it altogether**! To do this Daniel would still quit cold-turkey, stop buying, botting or putting cigarettes in his mouth. He would *not* use nicotine patches (as they keep the craving alive – whereas quitting cold-turkey means the actual nicotine cravings are gone after a few days). He would enjoy out-smarting his limbic system by slipping every urge, sensation, feeling, thought, image or memory related to smoking off into his periphery and instead he would focus much of his attention on the constructive activities (Step Four) of getting healthy and fit. Without any mentations about smoking, Daniel becomes a non-smoker immediately from the second he stubs-out his last cigarette. From that point, Daniel will describe himself as a non-smoker to both himself and others.

Many people believe that they cannot quit smoking because they have some sort of 'psychological' addiction, truly believing they just 'love' smoking (or drinking) and that they could not live happily in life without it. This is another complete fallacy. Nicotine is simply highly physically addictive (we have lots of acetylcholine receptors in our brains that recruit nicotine if it is available), and once these receptors get used to nicotine they like it delivered to them regularly. This leads people to develop mentations (of 'love' and 'neediness') around the addiction. But the reality is that as soon as the acetylcholine receptors adjust to no more nicotine, all the 'love' and 'neediness' mentations disappear, so long as all the mentations are quit along with physically stopping smoking. Daniel will find that quitting is

easy and any urges will disappear extremely fast (most of them after a few days) so long as all the mentations are quit *forever* at the same time. It will be like flicking a switch.

Step Four involves Daniel immersing his attention at all times on constructive pursuits that he enjoys, and activities that will upskill, benefit and progress him forwards in life. Daniel will think about what skills he would like to have more of in his brain, because whatever he focusses his attention on he knows he will learn. He will also try to take up constructive pursuits that punch above their weight and benefit him *most* effectively.

For example, even if Daniel is a poor swimmer, when he quits smoking he might decide to take up swimming and join a swim squad where he can get good instruction. This way he will have to breathe out against the positive pressure of the water when he swims freestyle and this will improve his lung capacity helping to expand and 'unglue' his gummed-up and damaged alveoli, assisting his lungs in trying to heal. He can also decide to have a very pleasant sauna after his swim, and do some deep breathing in the sauna with long exhalations that will both calm him down (helping his anxiety) and encourage more blood circulation to his lungs (and body generally), also aiding in healing.

Regular swimming (perhaps 3 times per week) will help Daniel become *genuinely* fit and healthy. It will assist in cardiovascular fitness, strength and flexibility. He will meet a new group of people that he can connect with and learn from, and this may help him slowly disengage from body-building and its greater emphasis upon appearance and muscle gain irrespective of cardiovascular fitness or flexibility.

It doesn't matter if Daniel has no interest whatsoever in swimming at the beginning, because the more he learns about swimming and the better he gets at it, the more he will become *fascinated* by the detail of how to really do it well. Over time, swimming will become more and more incorporated into his self-identity and he will learn to 'love' it.

This brings me to another fallacy. Many people believe they somehow just *innately* 'love' particular pursuits in life, like 'I just love reading', 'I just love going to the movies', 'girls just love fashion', 'I'm just passionate about social enterprise', 'I'm just passionate about cooking', 'boys just love footy', 'I just love food', 'girls just love pink', or 'I just love dogs'), as though they were born to it. However, the reality is that we must *learn* to love.

Recall that we have absolutely zero dendritic spine activity in-utero and we only start to develop dendritic spines within the first few days *after* birth. From then onwards, we basically learn to 'love' whatever is positively reinforced. This does not make the 'love' any less real it just makes it contingent upon our (sometimes random) experience and upon the prevalent social values that we absorb through learning.

This means that while we all feel (to ourselves) very much like innate 'individuals', the reality is that we are almost entirely *socially* constructed via our massive capacity for learning. For example, although new-borns have enormous potential, there is zero evidence that they can do anything more than react to a couple of reflexes (withdrawing from painful stimuli or turning towards the breast for suckling) which is even less than slugs can do. On the other hand, the colossal advantage of humans is our capacity to learn with highly flexible and large brains, which contrasts strongly with the prescriptive or 'innate' construction of slugs, where they enter the world being able to do almost everything they need in order to survive.

With practice humans can learn to love pretty much anything. The more we know about something, the more synapses we build, and the more likely we are to be positively reinforced because we feel good within ourselves about having lots of skills and knowledge. Being skilful and knowledgeable also moves us higher up social hierarchies, making other people more likely to positively reinforce us in our behaviour via praise, status and seeking-out our knowledge on our specific skills. The more this happens, the more *central* the skills become to our self-identity, and the more inclined we are to *mistakenly* believe that they are 'innate' and we have 'always' loved them.

Over time, Daniel has come to believe he 'loves' body-building and regards it as central to his self-identity. It is important therefore that when he starts to move away from it that he either has in place or quickly builds other constructive skills that he enjoys and which will replace any gap in his self-identity left by gradually doing less body-building. He doesn't need to immediately stop body-building altogether (as there are some constructive aspects to it like feeling stronger and meeting people) but there are definitely also some clear negatives like excessive focus on appearance, muscle bulk and miniscule levels of body-fat, that *drive and consolidate* many of his problematic behaviours.

As Daniel slowly moves away from body-building he will take up interspersing his 3 times a week swimming with some very light interval jogging (that he gently builds up as his body is able to tolerate more), and this will provide some weight-bearing exercise, that will re-strengthen the bones that smoking has weakened.

Very importantly, Daniel needs to build more career-type skills especially as he moves away from body-building and security work. He would initially maintain his security work (which has flexible hours and can financially support him) while he commits to some full-time university studies (or even a bridging course into university) where he might undertake some business, arts, statistics and law units with the view to applying further down the track to enter the police force, since Daniel expresses an interest in a career with the police. Even if Daniel is not successful with entering the police force he will have gained a broad range of units under his belt (and hopefully a degree) that will equip him well for many other careers.

Even a study period of 1–2 years will help Daniel achieve vastly increased chances of success while applying for the police force, as it will enormously sharpen his literacy, numeracy, abstraction, comprehension, computer and organisational skills which will be tested in the entry process. Also, after a reasonable period of swimming and jogging, Daniel will be unlikely to have any difficulties with the health/fitness component of his application.

Daniel will also need to have some 'on hand' constructive activities to remind him to apply when he gets anxious sensations, feelings and urges to back to old, problematic behaviours, like chasing his girlfriend, binge-drinking, smoking or gambling. He will make a list of these and write them on a card that he carries in his pocket to pull out and choose from whenever necessary.

It will include things like doing some mental maths in his head, making up a rhyming poem, listing in his head all the animals he can think of that start with a particular letter, naming as many countries as he can think of, reading the newspaper, doing a crossword puzzle, playing a digital game on his phone, getting down for 40 push-ups, listening to talk-back radio (especially if driving), doing some hard yoga poses, watching a difficult documentary on screen or TV, having a 'vigorous' conversation with someone, doing some study, engaging in a brain-demanding work task, going for a jog or swim or bike-ride, or playing the guitar (since Daniel has expressed an interest in learning to play the guitar).

Daniel will diligently apply his four ST steps. For example, every time Daniel gets an urge to check his mobile for messages from his girlfriend, Daniel will not allow himself to check (Step One); he will stay below 3/10 by doing a body-flop (Step Two); he will gently slip off to his periphery and show complete disinterest in the urge to check his phone or any other mentation associated with it, like sensations, other feelings, thoughts, images or memories (Step Three) and instead, Daniel will immerse himself 100% in his chosen constructive activity of perhaps, playing a song and singing along on his guitar (Step Four).

Daniel will also keep in mind the 'six aspects of self' and commit to incrementally improving himself slowly over time in each of these categories: Over time Daniel will obtain more and more 'meaning' in his life by increasing his contribution to the world through extending his career with extra study and application. Daniel will also genuinely improve his health and fitness through quitting smoking, quitting binge-drinking, taking up swimming, jogging, yoga, bike-riding, and developing a more relaxed and sustainable nutritious way of eating (80–20), with zero vomiting, laxatives, and diuretics. Daniel will also calm himself down mentally with the body-flop ensuring he is always staying below 3/10 and he will *only* pay attention to constructive mentations that he intends to build more of in his brain, while at the same time making sure he slips off all unhelpful material (like gambling) into his periphery.

Daniel will also increase his hobbies and interests by taking up guitar, taking up swimming, bike-riding, yoga, jogging and by joining 'interest clubs' at university. Through all of these pursuits, Daniel will extend his wider social networks meeting a wide range of people, many of whom will be well-skilled and able to help Daniel learn. Over time, Daniel will improve his relationships with people who he wants to be close to, especially his children and his ex-wife. Daniel will try to equalise his relationship with his girlfriend, attempting to eliminate her aggressive behaviours, and the extent to which he will fail or be successful at this will depend upon how well Daniel learns assertion skills.

PART FOUR

HOW DO I MAKE MY CHANGES PERMANENT?

CHAPTER TEN

ENSURING YOU NEVER GO BACK THERE

Perhaps just take some moments now to ponder whether you are truly ready to take charge over your brain and your life with ST. Are you ready to stop being a victim and get properly into the driver's seat? If you have doubts, then go back and re-read parts of this book until you feel sure you will do whatever it takes to stop paying attention to useless, time-wasting, debilitating mentations that suck the life energy out of you.

Understand that making the clear, unequivocal and courageous decision to quit paying attention to all that anxiety and negativity is fun! And a huge relief! It is a decision that you can make **right now**. You have the knowledge and you have the skills from reading this ST guide. Right now is the time that you can decide to quit your anxiety *forever*.

Right now is the time to start *genuinely living* the rest of your life. Stop being passive in your own life; stop pleasing others and dancing to their tunes; for once in your life, **commit to yourself**. There is no cavalry coming to rescue you. **You must save yourself.** You have **everything** you need inside you, all the necessary bits and pieces to **enable you to take charge** and stop all the nonsense. It is **your** brain, and **you can decide what you put in it!** It is **your** habit and *only* **you** can decide to change it. It is **your** brain, and **you** are **fully in charge** of it from now on!

Let yourself feel the **relief** and the **responsibility**! No more times of endless worrying. No more feeling like a captive victim to your own brain. You can **decide** to simply ignore all of the anxiety and all of the negativity. What a pleasure to have so much more time to spend pursuing all those wonderful, constructive things you used to dream of doing years ago!

It is entirely **your choice**. You can devote your whole life and billions of synapses to nonsensical worries, distress, fear, anger, addiction, paranoia, passivity, powerlessness and victimhood, **or** you can devote your life and billions of synapses to **constructive** choices that lead you out of that abyss. It is your life and therefore your choice, but know that you have the power **within you to save yourself**. All that is required is a **clear decision** to stop paying attention to all that unpleasant and horrible rumination! In a way, there is nothing really to give up. After all, it is *so* unpleasant to ruminate, it locks you down, makes you stagnate and fester. It is so much more fun to think constructively! It will be the **biggest joy of your life** to make the decision to save yourself!

Even if initially hundreds of times a day, stupid, scary little mentations try to pop into your mind, you can just wave them all away. No real effort required! Simply ignore all the annoying chatter coming up from the limbic system, creating waves of nausea, feelings of dread, quickened heart rate, flatness of mood, shakes, blushes, sweats, threatening thoughts or images – **simply disregard them**. After all, you know you are **bored to the back teeth** with them.

After reading this ST guide, you also know now that they are just CRF-driven misunderstandings. Unless you are terribly unlucky, your life is **not** at risk, you have just had an upsetting stressful life event. You can trust yourself to deal with the event **constructively**! You now have better and more important things to think about (like your next constructive activity or project).

All you have to do is decide to slip anything you would prefer became a **smaller** part of your brain, off to the side, into your periphery – take it out of your focussed attention. It can be vaguely there, but you are certainly not going to be paying attention to it – **it will never be in the front of your mind again!** After all, who could be *bothered* worrying about it anymore! Such a waste of time! Just a CRF-driven imaginary threat!

On the other hand, anything you would like to become a **bigger** part of your brain (like constructive pursuits) you can bring strongly into your focussed attention. The more you focus your attention on them the better. In fact, **constructive** approaches are **all** that you will ever again focus upon, for the rest of your life. The solution to stopping yourself from spiralling further down that deep abyss **is that simple**!

Being constructive the ST way does not mean that you will never again reflect upon your mistakes, or be remorseful. In fact, the opposite is true. ST teaches you to reflect **more** upon your own views, opinions and mistakes (by applying robust self-critique techniques), but that critique and self-reflection is **always** done in a constructive manner.

Endless, guilt-driven or global worrying actually let you off the hook. They stop you from having to take specific responsibility; it allows you to just ruminate on what a **totally** terrible person you are while doing absolutely nothing about changing your behaviour since you are so terribly terrible, where on earth would you start – your terribleness is just too overwhelming!

Instead, ST *requires* the taking of proper responsibility. Constructive reflection will be along the lines of 'I behaved badly, I did x, y and z. I now realise that was a mistake and I am sorry and remorseful for my error. The best I can do here is realise that mistakes are an opportunity to learn, and I will *make sure* I learn from my error – it will not be wasted. So next time I'm in a similar situation I will do a, b and c instead and see if that produces a better outcome'. Beyond taking proper responsibility, apologising, and determining to change our behaviour in future (all constructive behaviours), there is no further need to ruminate and dwell upon our own failings, and we can move on to the next constructive pursuit.

This approach results in small, incremental but continuous change. It drives **constructive** problem-solving that, over time, moves us closer and closer towards better outcomes for both ourselves and others (win-win solutions). ST makes us accountable for our behaviour, *not* because of externally imposed rules but because of our own **internal standards**, holding ourselves accountable for our own lives. This all stems from one simple fact, which is that we have a frontal brain that we can teach to exert control over almost every aspect of our behaviour, including many of our brain behaviours or mentations.

THE IMPORTANCE OF SADNESS

Focussing henceforth on constructive mentations and actions only does not mean that you will never be sad again. Of course you will be sad. Sad things happen in life. But with ST you will deal with that sadness **constructively**. Instead of deflecting off and away from the sadness and into anxiety, anger, substance abuse, over-eating, depressive rumination or guilt, you will deal with your sadness **front on** and actually **be sad** and actually **cry**.

Crying is a constructive activity. Men need to do it just as much as women. Just like dreaming, laughing, sexual orgasm and taking specific responsibility, crying allows our brains to habituate and reduce overly-hyped up neural firing rates. Crying, like the above behaviours, holds our brains in sustained contact with sensations, feelings and other mentations we need to resolve at a physiological level. Bit by bit, crying gradually resolves sadness, healing and habituating our brains to that sadness.

When we experience a stressful life event there is usually some sort of 'loss' involved (like losing an intact family when divorce happens, or losing the chance to have a career in medicine if we do poorly in exams, or losing our health and capabilities if we develop a chronic illness). Loss makes us sad.

When we need to be sad, our brains throw up tiny little packages of sadness that are opportunities for us to cry and heal. We ought to notice them and take them. It is important we don't push these opportunities away and have a glass of whisky instead, or have an angry outburst or an anxiety attack. Then we have simply deflected away from the sadness. Humans are the only animals on the planet that cry tears and that is probably because we have highly complex, self-building brains that benefit from the calming effects of habituation.

This does not mean collapsing into tears next time you are at work and you feel frustrated and powerless, or dissolving into tears because things didn't go your way in an argument with your spouse. (These crying strategies might be more about losing control, collapsing and trying to apply indirect pressure for an outcome.) Instead, I am talking about facing the sadness of your own life, mostly in the privacy of your own home, giving yourself the time to have small, tiny cries as required.

If you feel that a cry is overdue, you might deliberately see a film that deals with similar issues as your stressful life event and take some tissues, or you might take a long soak in a bath and let yourself think about what you lost, or you might get out a photo album and reminisce, or talk to someone really close about how *sad* (not anxious or depressed or angry) you feel.

When we focus, cry, and let ourselves be sad about a real-life event we habituate little by little to the *specific* event. On the other hand, when we focus on the imaginary events that often fuel anxiety or depression we can continuously ruminate and shift our fear or depressive target from one frightening 'what if' scenario to another (since our brains are so flexible that our imaginations or lateralising capacity is almost infinite), thereby preventing us from ever properly achieving habituation.

Whenever you are sad, embrace those opportunities to cry, especially as they usually only last for a few moments. You will notice that once you have cried you will feel better and you will have healed a little bit more. Once you have finished crying, gently move your attentional focus onto your next constructive activity. Strangely, it is not even necessary to know exactly why you were crying, just let yourself cry when you feel the urge and your brain will calm down physiologically, quickly habituating and reducing feelings of internal agitation. You will find there will be times in life where you feel the need to cry a lot (say, if you lose someone close) and other times where you barely cry at all.

In my work, I notice that no-one ever tries to deflect away from happiness but that many people (especially anxious or depressed people) do try to deflect away from sadness. When we deflect away from sadness but have CRF-induced agitation from a stressful life event, it is easy to deflect our attention onto other agitations that easily capture our attention, like anxiety, dread, addiction urges, depression, jealousy, paranoia, body images issues, envy, guilt, and anger, which we often describe as 'emotions'.

However, it may be that sadness is the emotion requiring habituation whereas these others are perhaps more like 'learned strategies' that enable us to keep our focus *away* from sadness. For example, in my work, I often notice that the *intensity* of the anxiety often matches the intensity you might expect for the sadness of the stressful life event – yet the person is not even slightly focussed on the sadness. If this is the case, it may be particularly important to allow sadness to be felt and habituated, as it may help reduce the underlying fuelling of learned deflections.

Try to keep this in mind going forward with your own self-rescue and let yourself cry and be genuinely sad whenever an opportunity arises. Shortly, I will be talking about how in ST we want less overall focus on our internal mentations (like sensations and feelings), but sadness is the exception to this general rule. It is not that you need to be sad most of the time, it is just that when sad things happen (usually rarely), it is important not to deflect your attention away into other agitation strategies like anxiety.

Whatever you do, don't let yourself be put off by the idea of sadness and crying. When we need to cry, crying feels really good! It feels healing. Always remember, that crying about genuine sadness is highly constructive. It is probably the reason why many emotion-based psychotherapies (like psychodrama) can be effective, since these therapies connect people to their sadness and calm people down enough so that they can often move forward in their lives.

If you feel overdue for a cry, let yourself cry now. Cry about all the sad things that have upset you so deeply in your life. All the losses and disappointments. Don't worry if there are no tears. Sometimes when we have buried our sadness deeply for long periods it takes practise to learn how to cry again. Just continue with the crying motion and gradually over weeks or months the tears will return. Take your time – let the sadness come and let the relief come. Once you have cried for a few moments, take a few long, deep breaths and think about moving your attention onto another constructive activity.

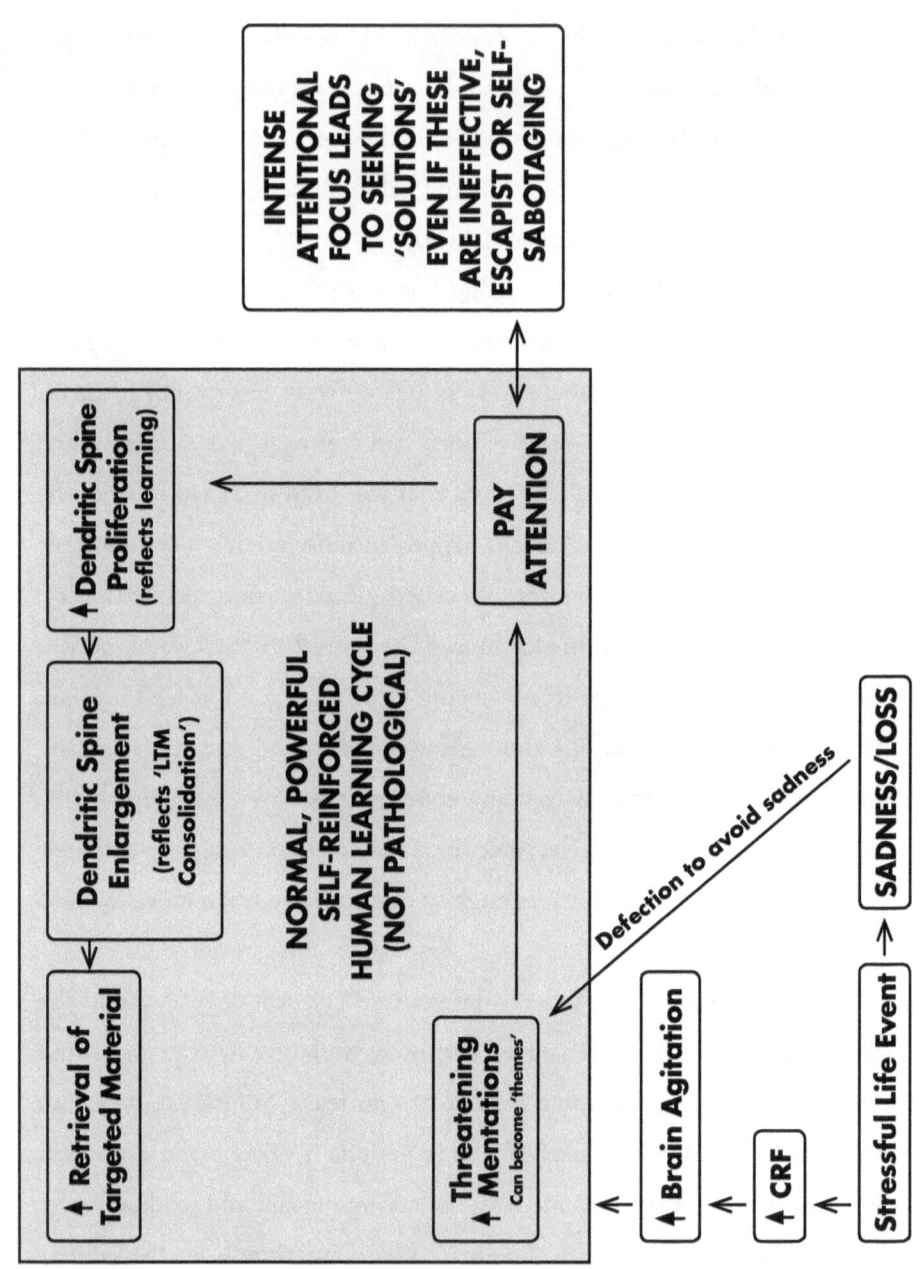

Experiencing sadness can be frightening so it is easy to deflect away from the sadness and instead pay attention to the threatening (and competing) mentations arising from CRF since they are of roughly equal intensity

In this case, your constructive activity is (hopefully) one of committing to ST and rescuing yourself from the abyss of anxiety and distress. So, do you feel ready? Eliminating enormous amounts of negativity and the distress that comes with that negativity seems to be a very good reason for making the decision to quit anxiety and take charge with ST. There will be no more hours of time-wasting and debilitating rumination; no more focus on despair and hopelessness; no more self-harming behaviours that sabotage your life. Making the decision to self-rescue is the **single most important** decision of your life. Remember, you have the tools.

Remind yourself of your four steps. For **Step One**, remember to write down which of your behaviours are ineffectual, dysfunctional and self-sabotaging. Ask yourself how a person would behave if they did not have your difficulty and mirror that behaviour. Make a list of all of your 'problem' behaviours and make the decision to stop them now, preferably all at once. If there are too many to quit all at once (or there are other practical limitations like requiring a slow withdrawal from sedative medications), then do a hierarchy or timeline so that you are absolutely clear about when you will quit other self-sabotaging behaviours. **Commit** to self-rescue and make a clear decision to stop the most important ones now!

Next, remind yourself of **Step Two**, and how it is **always** your job to stay below 3/10 no matter what is happening around you. This step means that even if you go into work and there is huge pressure to complete jobs, it is still always your job to stay completely calm, focussed and relaxed and below 3/10. You will be much more efficient in this state than if you allow yourself to get to 8/10 where you will feel out of control.

Recall the three aspects of the Body Flop exercise (settle and quieten the brain, dampening-down the noisy chatter of the limbic system; flop and soften the entire body releasing every muscle and tendon; and release and exhale all the inner emotional tension). Make sure you use the Getting Real exercise and don't overestimate the severity of your anxiety compared with how difficult things could actually be in real life. Also, use the Whatever Happens exercise to help lower your physiological agitation. If you have not already done so, take yourself through these exercises now, writing your own version of the Whatever Happens exercise.

Then, remember **Step Three** where you determine to *never again* allow yourself to focus your attention on **any** self-sabotaging themes. Recall you have 100% control over ensuring these mentations are **off** your repertoire. Allow your synapses devoted to self-sabotage to degrade, break apart and retract, disappearing along with their ability to influence your mental life. Stop giving them a vote!

Make sure you differentiate between focussed attention and peripheral attention. Remind yourself (from Chapter Six) about some of the different 'types' of mentations like sensations, feelings, images, memories or thoughts you might prefer to remove from your mental repertoire. Simply slip these destructive mentations off into the periphery before they 'stick' while they are still half-formed, and you only have a vague awareness of their content. Recall that no force is necessary, just slide them off gently. You will find that you quickly come to enjoy out-witting your self-sabotaging limbic system.

Adopt an attitude of complete disinterest and boredom to the old, useless mentations. Remember to slip the **whole package** off into the periphery including sensations, feelings, thoughts, images or memories. This whole package of mental events happens with any theme you are trying to eliminate, be it anxiety, depression, anger, addiction or whatever.

Extinguish them all by **sheer boredom** and slippage to the periphery, ensuring they are never again in your focussed attention. Recall, you are not a powerless child who 'wants' or 'tries' to slip-off these self-sabotaging mentations. It is that you **intend** to do it and **will** do it. **Right now and forever!** You will get better and better at this mental control, **very quickly**.

In fact, you can tell your limbic system regularly and quite sternly, to 'not even bother throwing up these useless, boring mentations because you will **never be interested again**!' Say this to yourself quite frequently, especially at the start and during any later stressful life events where there might be a slightly stronger urge to re-engage with these old ruminations. Show a level of utter contempt for the nonsense your limbic system throws up. Enjoy defying it!

Next, remember that **Step Four** helps you achieve Step Three. Step Four shifts your attentional focus away from self-sabotage, anxiety, worry, catastrophe, fixation, anger, hostility, stubbornness, envy, hatred, bitterness, psychosis, or addiction and allows you to focus attention instead onto constructive pursuits.

Recall that going forward, you will be building a brain packed full of constructive skills and mentations. You will be spending huge amounts of time on constructive activities, in fact, **all of your time**!

Keep in mind, that while, we cannot eliminate stressful life events, we can ensure we always deal constructively with them as adults. If we are sad, we need to be constructive and let ourselves cry here and there (as much as needed), allowing ourselves to habituate to that sadness. Once we have had a little cry, then we can move onto our next constructive activity and focus on that for a while.

Recall that initially when we start with ST, it is easier if we choose fairly brain-demanding constructive pursuits and pay strong and focussed attention to them like mental maths, crossword puzzles, Sudoku puzzles, rhyming poems, talk-back radio, complex TV documentaries, reading non-fiction, vigorous conversations, harder physical exertion such as jogging, swimming, vigorous bike-riding, push ups, or completing intricate work tasks that demand sustained attention.

If you ensure high levels of mental control and *decisively* remove useless content from your repertoire, then within a few days, things get a lot easier. As the urge diminishes to go back into the old, useless rumination, then gradually introduce some more lay-back constructive activities like watching less demanding films, reading novels, going for relaxed walks, doing relaxed housework, going for slow bike-rides, chatting with friends, giving or receiving massages, calmly (and in an exploratory manner) thinking about possible career moves, cooking delicious and nutritious food or simply lying in the gentle sun googling interesting internet sites.

The key is to always stay *focussed* on the pleasure or actions of whatever it is you are doing no matter how undemanding the task. While these more lay-back constructive activities require less brain, they can still be entered into fully and with sheer enjoyment. These very relaxing constructive pursuits will still incrementally progress and propel you forwards in life by advancing each of the six aspects of self. While there are times where we may like to progress rapidly in life (like when we want to learn a new skill fast), there are plenty of times where it is sufficient to make small, incremental and continual progress. All these small advances add up, accumulating over time into significant progress that is certainly a massive improvement upon entrenched anxiety where there is frequently stagnation or deterioration.

GOING FORWARD

Amazingly, your brain will change almost immediately at a neurological level in response to your clear decision to immerse in ST. If you are genuinely persuaded by ST, you will have already built many hundreds of thousands (and probably millions) of new synapses specifically devoted to concepts like taking responsibility for the content of your own brain, taking charge and not being a passive victim, the importance of self-rescue, and the importance of maintaining a constructive focus of attention.

If you apply ST diligently, within a few days (and sometimes immediately) you will think and feel very differently, as though you have been liberated from prison – and of course, you have! No more hours wasted ruminating endlessly about tedious, boring, and imagined threats. You now know that rumination is a **choice** over which you can exercise voluntary control. Your frontal brain can simply **decide** to stop ruminating. You have the steps and all the exercises within the steps to help you achieve this outcome.

Instead of hours wasted ruminating, you now have time to spend enjoying constructive activities, things you have always wanted to pursue except you never had the time. Now you are no longer a captive prisoner of worrying and paying attention to all that negativity, you have hours every day to spend on advancing your life in your desired direction. What courses have you always wanted to pursue, what sports, what hobbies, what social events – how can you make a real difference to the world, now that you have freed yourself from the prison of worry?

Due to our high levels of cognitive flexibility, as we continue with ST, after only a few months, we have literally billions of new constructive pathways dominating our mental life, requiring barely any effort on our part to retain the new equilibrium. We now **genuinely** think differently (at a synaptic level) and we have climbed out of the all-consuming abyss of anxiety!

STAYING OUT OF
THE ABYSS OF ANXIETY

Ensuring that anxiety is never a problem again is actually not so hard. Here are a few guidelines, apart from your four steps, to help you. The first guideline is, **never get complacent.** While building billions of constructive synapses is exhilarating, we must also be aware of how to maintain this new, liberated brain state in the longer term. While we can, of course, relax and be carefree for the most part we still need to **always** know at some level that problematic habits can be regained. This is just the flip-side of brain flexibility. What has been built can be eliminated and what can be eliminated, can also be re built.

While there may have been hundreds of millions of synapses devoted to a single concept in our brains (for example like a 'fear of cancer'), by not paying attention to the fear we will eliminate almost all of the devoted synapses. As a result, after a few months we will rarely ever have a mentation about it, and when we do have the occasional one, it is likely to feel 'vague' and it will be very easy to resist focussing on it.

But while we experience rare and occasional mentations, this tells us that there are still some synapses materially (or physically) present producing those mentations. It may only be shreds of the old fear of cancer that are still retained on just a few thousand deteriorated neural pathways here and there, barely ever bothering us, but those neural pathway still nonetheless, physically exist, and therefore they can be reactivated if we ever start to focus our attention upon them again.

So never forget this, especially when you experience future stressful life events, because CRF will activate some of those old, useless neural pathways and bring forth some old (and new) anxious, depressive, angry, addictive or self-sabotaging mentations. Remember that CRF makes mentations feel very intense and frightening, so we can easily start to refocus on them again. Even so, while it is important to be *aware* of this, there is absolutely no need to be afraid of it!

Simply *know* that if in the future you have some scary mentations 'pop' into your mind, it is just additional CRF-induced neural agitation related to the new stressful life event that is driving these 'extra' disturbing thoughts. According to ST, there is absolutely nothing wrong with you. There is no pathology. There is no 'return' of pathology (since there was none to begin with).

Always remember that this CRF-induced agitation happens to everyone on the planet. Just make sure you respond the ST way. That is, completely ignore any disturbing thoughts, feelings, sensations, images or memories and enjoy doing so! Simply decide **not to go there mentally! Ever again!** Not even for a second! After all, these ruminations are too *boring* to bother with. Just allow these silly mentations to die a natural death by keeping your attentional focus on other constructive pursuits. Take them out of your attentional spotlight and watch them diminish rapidly and they will cause you no further problems.

Also, be aware that often when people quit smoking they have a dream or two maybe a few months down the track where they dream they have 'accidentally' out of habit stuck a cigarette in their mouth and lit it, only to awake in horror! Of course, they feel immediate relief as soon as they realise it was only a dream and they have not actually re-started smoking.

A similar thing can happen with quitting anxiety, where usually after a few months of not having any anxious thoughts, the person suddenly thinks something like 'it has been absolutely brilliant not having any anxiety. OMG! Wouldn't it be awful if my anxiety came back?'

Sometimes, having had such little anxiety for several months means people may have temporarily 'forgotten' the crucially important ST requirement to keep their focus away from their anxiety. As such they might 'accidentally' re-indulge in worrying about 'how awful' it would be if their anxiety came back, thereby awakening it from the dead. This does not happen to all people, but it is reasonably common.

Please note that this is just the 'last hurrah' of the limbic system and **make sure you don't fall for it**!

Since the thought of 'accidentally' going back there will feel very intense because you *now* know how good life can be without anxiety, it is important, especially at this point, that you do not indulge the limbic system whatsoever. Immediately, slip the mentation off to the side and engage straight away in a fairly brain-demanding constructive task.

Of course, after several months of no anxiety mentations this sudden thought about anxiety coming back is likely to shock and frighten you, catching you by surprise. It may also feel fairly powerful, particularly as you will be strongly aware of what is at stake now that you know *just how good* life can be without anxiety.

Your limbic system, sensing this vulnerability, may try to kick in hard and make several attempts during the same day or the next day to try and get you to pay attention again onto the anxiety. So long as you know how to respond the ST way by ignoring and shifting any anxious mentations off into your periphery then you will be fine. In fact, *enjoy* defying your limbic system. Know that it is in its last death throes and that it cannot trick you. Gently let these resurgent mentations die a natural death over the next day or two and you will be back better and stronger than ever!

The second guideline is to **stop over-focussing on mentations generally.** People, especially in Western culture, often think they ought to pay lots of *inwards* attention, especially to their feelings. In therapy people are often encouraged to 'get in touch' with their emotions (constructive and destructive) as though this is an essential aspect of mental health and insight.

As you would be aware by now, ST advocates a different approach. Don't bother getting in touch with mentations that give you and others poor outcomes like anger, guilt, hostility, irrationality, envy, urges for violence, stubbornness, resentment, closed-mindedness, depression, addiction urges, rage, paranoia, meanness, or anxiety – scrap them! Instead, in ST when we do focus on mentations (which is much less often) we only focus on the constructive ones, that give ourselves and others good outcomes like calmness, kindness, rationality, open-mindedness, logic, compassion, curiosity, specific self-critique, flexibility, sadness/crying (as required), friendliness and boldness – so we keep these!

However, over time, if we use ST consistently, we notice that we gradually develop less attachment *generally* to our own mentations. They seem less essential to us, as though we have gained some distance from them. (This is because we start to focus more on what we **do** in the world, outside of ourselves.) Also, as time passes, we really start to grasp just how highly flexible our mentations are. Now that we are often not paying attention to them, we notice they come and go, they are transient, and they may be full of all sorts of nonsense. We become more aware that they need only have very little (or no) impact. We can take them or leave them, and we nearly always ought to leave them!

We don't need to be constantly looking inwards, examining and exploring our mentations as though the 'truth' or some 'innate wisdom' or 'true self' resides there. It does not: we are born with zero dendritic spine activity. There is no 'innate' knowledge as far as we know scientifically. We are what we learn; and we can learn whatever we pay attention to. We simply attach our 'sense of self' to whatever dominates our attention in the longer-term. This longer-term attentional focus gives us a sense of stability which we often mistake for having a 'true self' but it is really just that we have been practising those mental behaviours for years or decades so they *appear* true to 'our nature'.

While many parts of our brains lack flexibility, our 'sense of self' is *not* one of them. In fact, our mentations are **the** most flexible parts of our brains. Consequently, self-identity is as fluid or as viscose as we decide. Our 'sense of self' can become whatever we decide to learn.

In keeping with this, we need to let go of stubbornly held, rigid, categorical views of self-identity (like 'I'm a good person' or 'I am a bad person' or 'I'm an anxious person' or 'I'm an angry person') which keep us in rigid categories and frequently hold us back from being truly open-minded and assessing each behaviour on its merits and specific context. It is nonsense that there are innately 'bad' people. There are people who have had 'difficult' lives and have learnt problematic strategies to survive, but in the end we can all decide to change our behaviour and our mental behaviours and therefore our sense of self.

Even the concept of 'intuition' is not some biologically-determined or God-given, inner wisdom. In the end, intuition boils down to well-practised mental habits, similar to 'procedural memory' which is developed, say, after years of driving a car and we are so practised that we do it 'automatically'. However, just as some drivers have learnt good habits in their procedural memory, others have not. Intuition is no different. In life we learn some mentations that are helpful and some that are not, and intuition is as likely to be helpful as it is unhelpful. Any actions to come out of 'intuition' ought to be assessed on their rational and logical merits, and not assumed to have magical power conveyed through some sixth sense.

In short, stop looking inwards for received wisdom. Often our inner mentations are just old, useless relics from our past, reflecting outdated and ridiculous views and unchallenged prejudices. Or they may be new mentations to which we are simply paying too much attention. In either case, we can simply decide at any moment to sever our self-identity from them and locate our new identity in broader and more fluid concepts that encourage progress, like open-mindedness, rationality, calmness, contextual kindness, mental flexibility, boldness and curiosity. So, perhaps instead of thinking of yourself as an 'anxious' person, you could scrap that idea and instead decide that you are an 'open-minded, kind, smart and bold person' and behave accordingly going forward in your life.

The third guideline is **to not expect perfection or demand 100% guarantees of safety.** Perfection or 100% guarantees for safety are like the demands of a child or victim not willing to accept reality. Sometimes devastating things happen in life and we must face them and do the best we can in the circumstances. One thing that is sure though, is that the less you perceive yourself as a victim, the better you will deal with any devastation. By filling your mind full of constructive skills and knowledge in ST you have the best chance of being safe in a rapidly-changing world. On the other hand, the stagnation and withdrawal that easily occurs with anxiety will quickly make your skills out of date.

Also, as humans, we all have highly flexible and responsive brains. So, don't expect that once you make up your mind to stop anxiety that you will never have another anxious feeling or sensation again. Of course you will. Your mind has been practicing and learning anxiety probably for months or years, if not decades. There will also be some anxiety-provoking situations that arise here and there in your future. The point is that they need never *bother* you again!

While you may continue to have very occasional and rare anxious thoughts forever (just like if you quit smoking), once you stop paying attention they have barely any impact since they are so easy to dismiss and they only occur very rarely, maybe once or twice a year or perhaps once every five years or even less. This will simply depend on how much you have practised your anxiety and how willing you are to decisively quit practising it. The more decisively you quit it the fewer anxious thoughts you will ever have going forward.

Right from the moment of your clear decision to quit anxiety the ST way, you will feel liberated by your decision, since you will understand that the *frequency and intensity* of your anxiety in the future is down to you! You can pay attention to it or **not**! It will get bigger if you do; it will get smaller and smaller if you don't. It is **your choice**, totally within your control. You no longer need to think that 'it just takes me over'. **It doesn't.** You can decide to always stay in control of your mentations.

Like I did, you will start to **enjoy** slipping off to the periphery any type of anxious mentation, whether it be a sensation, feeling, image, thought or memory. Know that your limbic system is just trying to throw you a curved ball to trick you. Enjoy baiting your anxiety when you use the Whatever Happens exercise, where you engage your frontal brain to take the brakes off your hyper-rigilance: **come on anxiety, go your hardest, do your worst, give it everything you've got!** Laugh at it; learn every trick; never again be sucked in by it!

The final guideline is **to behave with integrity.** The more we can sever our identity from old, irrational, self-sabotaging mentations and stubbornly held views and, instead attach our identity to broader and more liberating concepts like rationality, kindness, open-mindedness, calmness and curiosity then the more we can see **beyond** ourselves. **We look inwards**

less, and start looking outwards more.

When we are **less** caught up in our own misery, we get **more** distance, objectivity and clarity. We start to see our own and others' behaviour more clearly. Even when we use specific self-critique and are looking inwards, we do it constructively with objectivity, as though we are looking outwards at another person. Even when we allow ourselves to be sad and cry we are rational and objective about it. We know that *not* crying would encourage us to deflect into other problematic behaviours like getting drunk, getting angry or getting anxious. So we make the rational decision to cry and heal whenever necessary.

In ST we are no longer captive to our often messed-up and confused inner world. We deliberately place our attentional focus **beyond ourselves** (onto constructive activities), and in so doing we actually fix up our inner world by allowing destructive synapses to die a natural death due to lack of attention. In effect, we can create a **new start** to our lives.

This new start can make us and the world a better place, which is a genuine win-win. In ST our focus remains nearly always on the constructive behaviours we are trying to accomplish. There is no requirement to worry about what we think, sense, feel, imagine or remember. We slip whatever we want to minimise off to the periphery. Instead nearly all of our attention is on what we **do** in the world, on **how** we behave.

When we behave with **integrity** we keep ourselves honest. Through specific self-critique we acknowledge if we are lying to ourselves, or letting ourselves off the hook, or not taking proper responsibility, or being weak, passive, addicted, anxious or hostile, or if we are not taking proper charge of our lives. And we **change our behaviour in response**.

The more we behave with integrity, the less genuine need there is to look internally and self-critique, entering us into a truly liberating learning cycle. This frees up our time from internal examination, and allows us to direct our attention outwards onto the constructive pursuits that will make this world a better place for everyone.

The time has come now to end the talk and properly *require* something of yourself. No more delays, you have the knowledge and the skills. It's time to call yourself to account and command self-respect. You can do it! Change your behaviour and change your brain. No more useless worrying. No more self-sabotage. Dig deep, and insist on it! You have the power to create your own future, to **take charge** of your life going forward. **Right now** is the time to commit to **permanent** and **comprehensive self-rescue** through ST!

APPENDIX

THE NEUROLOGICAL BASIS OF SMART THERAPY

ST builds on existing knowledge, adding its own important contribution.

EXISTING KNOWLEDGE

1. Stressful life events (SLEs) are known to be implicated in the onset of many DSM-V identified 'disorders' including anxiety, depression, anger, addiction, eating problems and psychosis.

2. Although many of these identified DSM-V 'disorders' are argued to be maintained by self-reinforcing cycles, the precise mechanism of their continuance has not yet been identified and they continue to be viewed as pathological 'disorders' within the mental health system.

NEW KNOWLEDGE ADDED BY ST

1. ST contends that the increased release of Corticotrophin Releasing Factor (CRF) following SLEs leads to increased neural discharge and agitation within the HPA axis and the amygdalae (where threat is detected and monitored) making it more likely that the prefrontal cortex (PFC) will pay attention. This increase in CRF occurs when all humans (and animals) are placed under chronic and uncontrollable stress.

2. ST claims that people who have come from more difficult backgrounds and have encountered more threat have already learned to be more vigilant and *threat-alert* at the time of the SLE and therefore pay closer attention to the agitating effects of increased CRF in order to monitor, body scan, check for patterns, compare with memories, and check contexts of symptoms, in an attempt to problem-solve and fix-up their distress. ST argues this is *normal* problem-solving behaviour and it is not pathological or dysfunctional in the usual sense.

3. ST identifies increased prefrontal selective attention (PSA) or focussed attention as the primary mechanism whereby normal transient distress becomes a self-reinforcing cycle (generally known as a 'disorder'). PSA is represented in the brain as synchronous neural firing which amplifies downstream, increasing the proliferation and stabilisation of dendritic spines (new synapses) and making the PFC pay even more attention. This process leads to the normal learning of PSA-targeted content

and to the consolidation of long-term memory (LTM), causing increases in 'spontaneous' and intentional retrieval of PSA-targeted mentations as neural circuitry is further reinforced. The content of PSA-targeted mentations is whatever is the focus of concentrated attention and may include mathematics, geography or anxiety thoughts, feelings, sensations, images or memories. In nearly 20 years of anxiety work, the author and developer of ST has never seen even a single, anxious person who is not exerting significant amounts of PSA onto anxiety mentations (usually for many hours every day).

4. While this book argues the case for anxiety, it can be observed in clinical work that attentional focus can equally be directed towards other 'themes' that arise from CRF agitation, including depression, anger, body image, paranoia, distress intolerance and many other mental themes. When threat-alert people experience any type of 'scary' mentation (whether that be anxious, depressive, angry or whatever), they become alarmed and then mentally scan for any other related material. With additional PSA, mental themes easily develop, initiating even more PSA via feedback loops, thereby consolidating themes over time.

5. In ST, anxiety is conceptualised as part of the normal learning process, that has been inadvertently reinforced by PSA, rather than as a 'disorder' or mental 'illness'. There is nothing at all wrong with the brains of anxious people: Their brains have simply been learning whatever they have been directed (by PSA) to learn. Where the target material is anxiety-related then that is what will

be learned. On the other hand, when neural reinforcement is stopped by reducing PSA, then anxiety-content is subject to the usual processes of memory erosion and decay over time. That is, with reduced synaptic traffic, synapses destabilise and break apart and dendritic spines retract, losing their input capacity. As the neural circuitry weakens, the urge to attend to problematic mentations also diminishes. In clinical practice, unless anxious people suffer another SLE, they hardly ever experience any urges to re-engage with the anxiety-related material after 6–8 weeks of stopping PSA and those few urges that remain are weak and easy to resist.

6. Since humans are such excellent problem-solvers, intense PSA or attentional focus on CRF-driven threat naturally leads to an urge to find 'solutions' to that threat. These 'solutions' might include over-eating for comfort, substance abuse to reduce agitation, self-harm to distract from mental pain, refusal to use the number 7 in case it causes a loved on to die, hair-pulling to calm distress, under-eating to bolster fragile self esteem, refusing to fly or drive in case of an accident or acting out aggressively when frightened.

Until we realise that it is *our own attentional focus that causes the continuance of our threatening mentations*, we can easily persist (since our 'solutions' often don't work) and become increasingly desperate in endlessly seeking solutions even if they are ineffective, misguided, escapist or self-sabotaging. As people become ever more desperate their 'solutions' can present as quite odd or even bizarre and they can gradually encroach and take over and destroy peoples' lives. For example, walking back and forth through doorways for several minutes or hours until they have a 'good' thought so that they don't 'develop cancer'.

Once people realise that it is only their focussed attention that causes the continuance of these threatening mentations (like developing cancer), they are more able to stop seeking out such misguided 'solutions'.

ABSTRACT

Anxiety causes high levels of distress in the population. Many biomedical researchers identify anxiety as an internal pathological disorder, driven by genetic predisposition and chemical imbalance requiring medication to correct. More behaviourally orientated researchers (ACT and BT) claim anxiety to be caused by dysfunctional avoidance that requires exposure and submersion in anxiety phenomena to habituate and recover. Other more cognitively orientated researchers (CBT) argue that anxiety sufferers have dysfunctional thinking patterns maintaining their anxiety. In contrast, Smart Therapy (ST) contends that anxiety is learned through the normal processes of learning and memory. According to ST, anxiety arises following stressful life events (SLEs) which cause increases in CRF, making the brain more vigilant to threat and giving rise to distressing physiological sensations. In response, *threat-alert* individuals who have encountered more past objective threat tend to pay greater attention to the troubling anxiety phenomena through over-worrying, body-scanning, visualisation and memory retrieval in an attempt to solve the problem and get the anxiety to go away. The problem is that more focussed attention or prefrontal selective attention (PSA) directs the brain to learn the targeted material (in this case, anxiety-related) more efficiently, and facilitates the consolidation of these memories. While this paper deals specifically with anxiety, it is worth noting that attentional focus can equally be directed towards other 'themes' that arise from CRF agitation, including depression, anger, body image, paranoia, distress intolerance and many other mental themes since the brain will learn whatever it is directed to learn via attentional focus. The neurocognitive processes arising from heightened attention manifest in the brain as synchronous firing of ACC–DLPFC, pyramidal and other neurons associated with learning and memory, which culminate in the rapid proliferation of new dendritic spines (learning) and the enlargement of existing dendritic spine heads due to immediate early gene activation, facilitation of protein synthesis and AMPA receptor proliferation thereby more effectively consolidating the learned material into long term memory (LTM) storage. Anxiety-related phenomena are then retrieved more readily leading to a self-reinforced cycle of anxiety that can be ongoing for decades. ST teaches people how to stop paying attention to their anxiety phenomena, thus enabling them to recover from all types of anxiety 'disorders'.

INTRODUCTION

Anxiety is a common clinical problem that affects up to 10% of Australians at some point in their lives, often leading people to feel overwhelmed and unable to cope (Andrews, Hall, Teesson, & Henderson, 1999). Anxious people spend hours each day worrying and panicking, causing major disruption in their lives. This paper attempts to outline the precise mechanism that turns normal transient anxiety into an ongoing self-perpetuating problem defined as an anxiety 'disorder' and it provides a practical response that seems to assist anxious people to regain control and resume their lives. The outlined approach has been successfully applied in more than one thousand anxious people in a centre devoted to anxiety over the past 20 years.

ANXIETY CAUSES AND MAINTENANCE

Despite any coherent evidence for neural pathology in anxious people, there has been a long history of research (Hettema, Prescott, & Kendler, 2004; Kendler et al., 1995; Schildkraut, 1965) which identifies anxiety as an internal pathological disorder, caused by genetic predisposition and/or a chemical imbalance requiring medication to correct. Other, more cognitively orientated researchers (Beck, Emery, & Greenberg, 2005; Salkovskis et al., 2000; Whittal & McLean, 1999) have argued that anxiety sufferers have irrational thinking patterns which maintain their anxiety. More recently, learning-based researchers in Acceptance and Commitment Therapy (ACT) arising from Behavioural Therapy (BT) frameworks have claimed that anxiety is caused by dysfunctional avoidance that requires exposure and submersion in anxiety phenomena in order to recover (Eifert & Forsyth, 2005; Hayes & Strosahl, 2004; Hopko, Robertson, & Lejuez, 2006). This paper argues that anxiety is not pathological, irrational, or dysfunctional and that it occurs as a result of the completely normal processes of learning and memory.

It is now widely accepted that there is a clear causative role for environmental stressors in the onset of the anxiety disorders (Evans et al., 2009; Fredman et al., 2007; Hicks et al., 2009; Klauke et al., 2010).

Moreover, as the severity of the stressful life event (SLE) increases, individual risk factors diminish and even the most emotionally stable individuals will succumb to anxiety if the event is sufficiently severe (Keane & Barlow, 2002).

Extensive literature from both animal and human studies has demonstrated that CRF is released in larger amounts during sustained stress, activating the HPA axis and the amygdalae (Holsboer, 2000; Blank & Spiess, 2009; Hauger et al., 2009). The ST model argues that SLEs are correlated with increased output of corticotrophin releasing factor (CRF) which in turn leads to high levels of brain agitation, manifesting as anxious, depressive, angry or obsessive mentations.

At specific promoter sites within the cell nucleus, immediate-early genes (IEG) are activated during chronic stress and code for the proteins required for increased production of CRF and the IEG *c-fos* has been observed in larger amounts within the hypothalamic-pituitary-adrenal (HPA) axis during chronic stress in rats and mice (Dorin, Zlock, & Kilpatrick, 1993; Peeters et al., 2002; Thompson et al., 2004). Primates given even low doses of intracerebral CRF show enhanced vigilance as demonstrated by increased eye gazing and with yet higher doses they show hyper-vigilance featuring increased escape and withdrawal behaviours (Dunn & Berridge, 1990). In drug-free humans with anxiety and depression there is an increase in CRF concentrations in the cerebrospinal fluid, hyperactivity of the HPA axis, a blunted release of ACTH, and pituitary and adrenal gland hypertrophy, all of which are consistent with CRF hyper-secretion (Owens & Nemeroff, 2007).

Evidence from the molecular biology and animal behaviour literature has shown that CRF has a direct effect upon neural activity in that CRF lowers the requisite threshold for neurons to fire – thus making them fire more readily, leading to increased activity in particular brain regions

(Lewis et al., 2002; Linthorst et al., 2002; Lowry et al., 2000). Page and Abercrombie's study (1999) for example found that the discharge rate of neurons in rats increased by 88% following injection of CRF. In particular, CRF causes increased amygdalae activation, in the specialised areas of the brain where threat is processed and monitored (Lesscher et al., 2008; Merali et al., 2008; Thompson et al. 2004). The amygdalae feature high densities of CRF receptors that communicate with widespread regions of the neural axis, readily activating multiple neurotransmitter systems. Moreover, direct injections of CRF into the amygdala produce anxiety behaviours in animal studies, and rises in endogenous CRF within the amygdalae can be measured during stress in rodents (Cook, 2004; Lesscher et al., 2008; Todorovic et al., 2007). Chronic uncontrollable stress in rats culminates in increased endogenous CRF in the amygdalae and synaptic proliferation in the hippocampus, which can both be reduced by administration of a CRF antagonist (Sandi et al., 2008).

THE MECHANISM THAT TURNS ANXIETY INTO AN ANXIETY DISORDER

Since CRF is known to increase neural firing rates, it follows that when the amygdalae and HPA axis are subjected to larger amounts of CRF that there is an increase in the neural firing rates within the limbic system and sensory inputs, culminating in more frequent and intense signals of 'bottom-up' salience in the capacity to detect threat. This increased biological salience would be expected to lead some people to respond 'top-down' with higher levels of prefrontal mental vigilance, especially in those people who have come from more fearful backgrounds and who, as a result, are already more readily attuned to fear and threat. This is because past memories and experiences are known to guide and inform current behaviour by focussing attention on salient material (Chun & Turk-Browne, 2007).

ST contends that this increased mental vigilance is achieved by exerting more prefrontal selective attention (PSA) towards anxiety-activating phenomena, leading to heightened attention towards anxious mentations, mainly thoughts, feelings, images, memories and bodily sensations. Anxious people tend to examine and monitor their own mental processes to determine whether or not anxious mentations are present and, if so, whether these are appropriate to the context. If sensations are found to be inappropriate to context, then anxious people are likely to further increase their PSA in order to explore and find a plausible reason for the presence of these troubling sensations.

In this way, PSA can be seen as a sensible, rational and normal attempt to ascertain the cause of the intense and distressing CRF-induced physiological phenomena (such as insomnia, lack of appetite, lowered mood, nausea, shortness of breath, accelerated heart rate, dizziness, shakes, derealisation, and dread) in order to get these sensations to go away. To this end, anxious people voluntarily bring their attentional focus to the job of monitoring and searching for patterns and contexts to try to make sense and understand the phenomena so as to fix it. Unfortunately, for anxiety sufferers this attempt at problem-solving their distressing feelings paradoxically results in increased anxiety symptoms over the long-term. Indeed, it is precisely the increased attentional focus (or PSA) directed towards anxiety mentations that turns normal transient anxiety symptoms into a persisting full-blown anxiety 'disorder'.

PROBABLE NEURAL CORRELATES OF ATTENTIONAL FOCUS

PSA is analogous to the Central Executive component of the working memory (WM) model proposed by Alan Baddeley (Baddeley, 2000; Baddeley & Hitch, 1974), thus 'top-down' prefrontal, selective attention is paid to salient stimuli while irrelevant stimuli are largely ignored. Attention is a powerful factor in normal learning and the consolidation of long term memory (LTM), and as the amount of sensory information that can be attended and processed at any one point time is much greater than our brains can realistically consolidate, large tracts of information are discarded and only stimuli with the greatest salience are selected for further processing. Shifting our attention voluntarily and bringing relevant information into a focussed 'spotlight' is very likely the means by which we differentiate between important and unimportant stimuli (Awh, Vogel, & Oh, 2006; Tootell & Hadjikhani, 2000).

In the primate brain, information of biological salience is received and activates the attentional system if signals are sufficiently strong to warrant attention. Essentially, this process is thought to involve the receipt of information from sensory inputs which are directed through the Reticular Formation and the Thalamic pathways which communicate bi-directionally between different brain systems, facilitating or inhibiting impulses. If these impulses are sufficiently intense, then specific parts of the PFC – namely the Anterior Cingulate Cortex (ACC) and the Dorsolateral Prefrontal Cortex (DLPFC) – are recruited in order to focus and sustain attention on relevant signals and suppress unwanted noise (Medalla & Barbas, 2009; Ure, Videla, & Ollari, 2009). Human studies using functional MRI show the ACC and the DLPFC as neural correlates for attention and executive control (Bunge et al., 2001), and demonstrate signal changes and synchronised neural firing in the cingulo-prefrontal (ACC–DLPFC) network during attention tasks and suppression of signal changes in posterior brain regions while attention is being focussed (Kastner et al., 1998; Kondo, Osaka, & Osaka, 2004).

ATTENTIONAL FOCUS, LEARNING AND LTM CONSOLIDATION

Many studies have shown that the firing rates of neurons are strongly dependent upon the focus of attention (Niebur, Hsiao, & Johnson, 2002; Steinmetz et al., 2000). Indeed, the Nobel prize-winning molecular biologist, Eric Kandel has established that attention ultimately regulates the function and configuration of neural network maps in mice. He has noted that while some neural maps in mice are prewired, such as vision, touch or smell, other maps, such as spatial maps are highly plastic. His work has shown that the long-term stability of spatial maps 'correlates strongly and systematically with the degree to which an animal is required to pay specific attention' (Kandel, 2006: 212). When mice are forced to attend, their spatial maps remain stable and the animals remember easily. Even ambient attention was shown to be sufficient to form spatial maps although these became unstable after several hours (Kentros et al., 2004).

According to Kandel, the PFC can be readily recruited for voluntary regulation so that after receiving a signal of biological salience from a distant area of the brain it can signal back and adjust the firing rate of those distant neurons, exerting top-down influence and altering biological salience (Kandel, 2006). In this way, the PFC through attentional focus is directing the brain as to what information is important to consolidate into memory and what information can be ignored and discarded.

According to ST, repeated attentional focus over time of precise anxiety-targeted material, would be expected to lead to specific learned fear themes that then become incorrectly labelled as discrete anxiety 'disorders'. For example, a person may excessively focus on fears of social embarrassment (social phobia) or of collapse (panic disorder) or of being unable to escape a threatening situation (agoraphobia) or of being a child molester (OCD) or of getting fat (anorexia nervosa) or be terrified of mice (specific phobia) or be mentally over-focussed on a past life-threatening event (PTSD). In each case there is simply a different focus of attention, frequently relating to either earlier brain-themes already practiced by the individual or to the type of SLE that initiated the CRF response, or both. For example where a SLE occurred where a teenager lost their parent to long-term illness, the teenager having already had time to practice themes around illness would be more likely to then go on to develop a full-blown hypochondriasis fear theme following the parental death.

In many ways it would make more sense to discard the labelling and diagnostic terminology of many of the discrete clinical mental conditions seen in diagnostic manuals and instead to understand them in the context of the over-arching brain mechanism of excessive PSA that directs the brain to learn whatever is attended to whether that be themes about anxiety, depression, eating, anger or paranoia. In relation to anxiety specifically though, this would help simplify matters enormously as well as solve the problem of some commonly observed anxiety fear themes that do not feature in either DSM-IV-TR (2000) or DSM-V (2013) since they do not fit neatly into the specified categories, such as fears of losing control ('what if I go mad and end up in a psychiatric ward') or fears of not trusting oneself ('how do I know if I am really here' or 'how would I know for sure whether or not I had sex with someone'). These fear themes would currently be diagnostically labelled as 'anxiety disorder not otherwise specified'. Indeed, labelling so called 'disorders' under their fear themes makes little sense because although humans share many common experiences and are therefore likely to share some similar fear themes, we are also capable of coming up with quite unique and imaginative themes wherever an individual brain and an unusual context of SLE warrants it.

Once individuals consistently employ PSA in response to biologically salient, scary CRF-induced phenomena, such as threatening sensations, feelings, thoughts, images and memories, then they will continue to selectively target biologically salient material for further processing and efficiently develop a self-reinforcing cycle of distress. This cycle of distressing rumination can become highly debilitating, taking up to 20 or more hours per day, preventing people from living productive lives.

Intense PSA onto threatening CRF-driven fear themes naturally leads to an urge to find 'solutions' since humans are such excellent problem-solvers. When we are distressed, we sensibly try and minimise our distress through 'solutions'. Such 'solutions' may include avoiding job interviews due to fear of negative scrutiny or avoiding touching door handles due to a fear of germs.

However, these 'solutions' can easily restrict our lives from normality and entrench 'illogical' brain connections. For example, refusing to touch door knobs in case 'we catch germs and get sick' means we never allow ourselves to take normal risks in life that would otherwise demonstrate that we are highly unlikely to get sick from touching door handles. Without this regular demonstration and learning experience and with continued PSA on both our fear theme (of getting sick from germs) and on our 'solution' (of not touch door knobs) we inadvertently strengthen the *incorrect and illogical* connection in our brains that it is only our avoidance of door knobs that stops us from getting sick. In fact, it is usually our immune system that prevents illness since we are continually in contact with large bacterial colonies irrespective of our usual efforts.

Still other 'solutions' like alcohol, smoking, medications or drugs can have their own problems, such as addiction cycles or reinforcement of the belief that we are 'unable to cope' without them.

DENDRITIC SPINES, LEARNING AND MEMORY

The recent development of multiphoton imaging techniques has enabled single synapses to be observed *in vivo* and dendritic spines have been observed to be independent, compartmentalised, micron-sized protrusions that serve as the postsynaptic component of most excitatory central nervous system synapses, 'popping up' or retracting on pyramidal neurons in the most plastic areas of mammalian brains relating to attention, cognition, learning and memory (Calabrese, Wilson & Halpain, 2006; Nagerl et al., 2004).

Due to their pliable, actin-rich cytoskeleton, dendritic spines are able to dynamically change shape within seconds and, even though new spines start out small, they represent functional synapses that can readily enlarge in an activity-dependent manner whereby low levels of stimulation lead to their retraction or shrinkage and higher levels of stimulation lead to the proliferation of new spines and enlargement of spine heads in existing spines (Kasai et al., 2010). Larger spine heads are more stable, and they tend to be maintained during sleep and their increased excitatory receptors are likely to represent LTM whereas small spines are able to be easily eliminated during sleep or strengthened by additional activity and are likely to represent learning (Kasai et al., 2003; Matsuo, Reijmers, & Mayford, 2008; Yuste, 2010).

Neural activity, environmental enrichment and skill training are known to accelerate the creation of new spines (Alvarez & Sabatini, 2007; Restivo et al., 2009;) and Long Term Potentiation (LTP) is known to both trigger the proliferation of new dendritic spines and to expand and enlarge the heads of established spines by the adding of more Actin-F and by additional excitatory receptor proliferation (Calabrese, Wilson, & Halpain, 2006; Matsuzaki et al., 2004). Increased and decreased dendritic spine size in the amygdale are associated respectively with the learning of fear or safety (Ostroff et al., 2010). Behavioural learning in birds has been found to cause rapid dendritic spine turnover at the time of learning, followed by dendritic spine enlargement and spine stabilisation within 24 hours after learning a new song (Roberts et al., 2010). Behavioural improvement in mice was found to correlate with the extent of dendritic spine remodelling following novel learning with the preservation of some new spines – thereby providing a structural basis for learning and memory retention (Yang, Pan, & Gan, 2009).

PAYING ATTENTION, SYNCHRONOUS FIRING, LEARNING AND LTM CONSOLIDATION

ST contends that it is the act of PSA that increases the proliferation, size and stabilisation of dendritic spines that represent learning and LTM of anxiety phenomena in the brain of anxiety sufferers. PSA is the crucial mechanism that turns normal transient anxiety into a persistent self-reinforcing anxiety 'disorder'. In the experience of the author having observed over a thousand anxious people within a dedicated anxiety clinic, excessive attentional focus onto anxiety phenomena is present with *every* anxious person and with *every* type of anxiety 'disorder' irrespective of whether or not there are other behavioural forms of avoidance, and it appears to be the key factor in both causing and maintaining the anxiety 'disorders'.

In the brain, the process of attention manifests as synchronous firing of a neural population that responds preferentially to attended stimuli (Constantinidis & Goldman-Rakic, 2002; Fries et al., 2001; Sakamoto et al., 2008). This synchronous firing can be induced by the sending of simultaneous action potentials to neurons within a relevant population nudging each neuron (that is already close to threshold) further toward attaining threshold and increasing the probability of simultaneous firing (Niebur, Hsiao, & Johnson, 2002). Indeed, it has recently been demonstrated that the synchronous firing that occurs during attentionally demanding tasks is initiated from higher-order neurons within the PFC (Buffalo et al., 2010; Gregoriou et al., 2009). It is likely that the ACC–DLPFC having received increased sensory stimuli due to increased neural agitation from CRF, then sends simultaneous action potentials to relevant neural populations increasing the likelihood of synchronous firing that reflects this heightened attentional focus.

Increased focussed attention and the synchronous firing it produces has been demonstrated to result in rapid enlargements of dendritic spines, creating more stable and responsive shapes (Harvey & Svoboda, 2007; Kasai et al., 2010; Tanaka et al., 2008) that ultimately produce more robust neural encoding of anxiety phenomena.

Once they have emerged, new dendritic spines release molecules which act as attractants, bringing axon fibres into close proximity to them and encouraging novel synaptic connection. Although dendritic spines form in related clusters (Fu et al., 2012) they are compartmentalised so that activation remains within the spine without leakage to other spines, effectively creating a specific, democratic one-vote per spine influence on dendritic input, which ultimately affects whether or not the axon will reach its all-or-none action potential and activate other neurons (Calabrese, Wilson, & Halpain, 2006).

Preferentially focussing attention affects pyramidal neurons which have the potential to encode and detect synchronous firing of neurons dispersed throughout the brain (Kasai et al., 2010; Tanaka et al., 2008). It has been demonstrated that when we focus attention, large populations of spiny neurons will show synchronous changes in the shape of their dendritic spines. This rapid enlargement of dendritic spines is very likely connected to actin polymerisation triggered by calcium and represents active learning. This rapid enlargement of spines precedes the long-term stability of spines which seems to require LTP, gene expression, protein synthesis and increases in glutamate receptor numbers that probably represent LTM (Kasai et al., 2010).

In relation to anxiety, it is likely that less PSA on anxiety phenomena results in fewer dendritic spines and those that are present will be less stable, making them less likely to form connections with other axons, thereby reducing summation effects for firing and weakening the overall neural circuitry associated with anxiety. When we fail to pay attention it is difficult to learn. Moreover, if we stop practising and retrieving information from LTM ultimately over time this information degrades, as synaptic connections receive less 'traffic' and associations become weaker. Paying attention matters, and even when neurons are stimulated and able to fire when under anaesthetic, animals do not show the ability to create dendritic spines when in this inert, unlearning state (Kaech,

Brinkhaus, & Matus, 1999). Similarly in foetal mammals, the immature form of dendritic spines known as filopodia are not active *in-utero* and only increase in density during the first week after birth when the animal first encounters its environment and starts to attend and learn (Zhou, Homma, & Poo, 2004).

Based on these findings, ST argues that anxiety is *not* pathological, and, not even really a 'disorder' in the common sense of the word. The brain is simply doing what it is good at, that is, learning and consolidating LTM because our attentional focus is directing it to do so. Then, as we consolidate LTM more and more over time thereby strengthening the neural circuitry, the more we will 'spontaneously' retrieve anxious thoughts, feelings, images, memories and sensations. This is no different to spending 10 hours a day focussing on mathematics which culminates in more mathematics thoughts 'popping into' consciousness. When anxious people spend hours a day attending to their anxiety (or depression, anger, body image or whatever) they will likewise retrieve more thoughts connected to these themes. The more thoughts people have relating to specific themes, the more likely they are to think of those thoughts and other related phenomena as part of their identity. People having many anxiety thoughts see themselves as 'anxious' people, as though this is intrinsic to their biological makeup and there is something defective or faulty about them personally. In reality, it is just that they are attending to anxious phenomena and this process is simply strengthening and consolidating the targeted material due to habitual practice: The neural circuitry doing *exactly* what it has evolved to do.

OVERVIEW OF THE PSA MODEL WITHIN ST

A significant SLE leads to an increase in CRF (which increases firing rates of neurons in the amygdalae and HPA axis) alerting the attentional system (ACC–DLPFC) that threatening stimuli ought to be attended to with higher priority. The ACC–DLPFC then signals a relevant population of neurons (i.e. in the case of anxiety, neurons involved in past fear learning) by sending each neuron an action potential that increases the likelihood of them all firing synchronously. This synchronous firing (reflecting PSA) leads to large spikes in post-synaptic excitation potentials which amplify downstream through summation (algebraically and temporally), increasing the likelihood of yet more synchronous firing. The more this neural circuitry is activated, the more the ACC–DLPFC (through feedback loops) sustains attentional focus, by generating additional action potentials to the specific neural populations. This increase in synchronous firing gives rise to: rapid increases in dendritic spine numbers; rapid enlargements in spine heads; rapid increases in excitatory receptor numbers (AMPA and NMDA); and enhanced probability of gene activation and protein synthesis occurring within spines – which are necessary for LTM consolidation. As this practice is repeated, the neural circuitry will be reinforced and these synaptic connections will be strengthened, making the encoded material (in this case, anxiety-related material) more likely to be retrieved and accessed. The person will thus subjectively experience an increase in anxious mentations (including anxiety sensations, feelings, thoughts, images and memories) as the neural circuitry is repeatedly sensitised through heightened attentional focus. LTM will be strengthened and consolidated through continual reactivation and retrieval. Over time practised fear-themes develop and strengthen, becoming increasingly threatening and leading to an urge to find 'solutions' to reduce distress. Often these 'solutions' are restrictive, ineffectual, escapist, addictive and self-sabotaging and they can become more desperate and encroaching over time.

Excessive attentional focus on all anxiety phenomena must be stopped or dramatically reduced in order to counteract this process and to achieve signal weakening.

In this way anxiety is simply conceptualised in ST as a brain habit that has been inadvertently reinforced (by PSA) rather than as a dysfunctional state or mental 'illness'. As neural reinforcement is stopped by diminishing PSA, the dendritic spines destabilise and retract, and as the neural circuitry weakens, the *urge* to attend to the problematic phenomena also gradually diminishes. The author has observed within her anxiety clinic that, as with stopping other habits, anxious people hardly experience any urges to re-engage with the anxiety-related material after about 6–8 weeks and those few urges that remain are weak and easy to resist.

However, it is necessary to stay out of all anxiety phenomena, including paying absolutely no attention whatsoever to anxious bodily sensations, feelings, thoughts, mental imagery or anxiety-related memories. (The exception to this advice is if there actually is a life-threatening situation; in which case the objective evidence for the threat is self-evident and there would be no doubts about the need to take action.) In everyday situations though, any anxious mentations are simply slipped off into our peripheral awareness and out of our focussed attention and complete disinterest is shown towards them. Attention is immediately redirected away from the anxiety phenomena onto constructive activities.

Although this approach of staying out of anxiety thoughts altogether may seem counter-intuitive – particularly in view of earlier Freudian approaches, and more recently in view of the notion that thought-suppression may cause a rebound response in targeted material – it nevertheless works exceeding well in practice. The excessive influence of the thought suppression literature may have, in itself, been partly created by earlier Freudian notions about risks of repression of the 'unconscious' mind. However, current neuroscience research would suggest, that while there are neural processes in the brain that can be thought of as 'preconscious' (whereby only with the strength of summation of neural firing will certain stimuli break through to become part of our conscious experience), there is little evidence of an unconscious mind in the Freudian sense of unresolved primal urges. In other words if the urge or biological salience was strong enough it would break through into conscious awareness and would not be an 'unconscious' influence.

Although the thought-suppression research may be seen as problematic for ST, this does not need be the case for several reasons. Firstly, there is considerable discrepancy within the thought suppression literature with some researchers finding that strong efforts to suppress thoughts resulted in an increased 'rebound response' in the thoughts targeted for suppression, and other, more recent research, finding no evidence of rebound at all (Belloch et al., 2010; Luciano & Gonzalez, 2007; Purdon & Clark, 2001; Salkovskis & Campbell, 1994; Tolin et al., 2002; Wegner et al., 1987). Indeed, some researchers have found that deliberate distraction, which has often been regarded as a form of thought suppression, was beneficial and led to fewer intrusive target thoughts (Luciano & Gonzalez, 2007). Secondly, where a rebound response is confirmed it is often the case that the evaluations were carried out too soon after exposure to the 'white bear or pink elephant' to be sure that any effects were enduring. Thirdly, in the thought-suppression experiments, participants are nearly always responding to strict and disciplinary instructions from the experimenters that would be expected to lead to *strenuous* suppression attempts. It is possible that *strenuous* attempts at thought suppression might reflect emotional urgency, fear, and the need to be hyper-vigilant, thereby activating limbic circuitry and increasing the propensity for prefrontal attentional focus and scanning.

In any case, ST discourages strenuous suppression techniques and encourages instead a complete *disinterest* in any anxiety rumination whatsoever, with higher cognitive efforts being devoted to achieving depth of concentration in relation to constructive life activities. It is interesting to note however, that even where anxiety-sufferers get this wrong on occasion and do strongly suppress their anxiety phenomena, although there may be a slight, brief rebound, the anxiety phenomena still gradually diminish over time as long as the client refuses to give their anxiety any consistent PSA.

In a way this is not surprising, since humans are good at suppressing unwanted information – every minute of every day we are inundated with intrusive stimuli yet we learn very effectively to block out unwanted noises, information, thoughts, feelings, and other distractions so that we can voluntarily concentrate on the task at hand. Over time, we learn to be highly effective at attending to what is important and in blocking out other intrusive stimuli. Most importantly, we manage to do this hundreds of times a day without creating any apparent long-term 'disordered' or 'pathological' thinking patterns.

Finally, there is a distinction that needs to be made between PSA and peripheral/ambient awareness or attention. For example, you can walk the same 3 km walk every day for 5 years but still be unable to recall the paint colour of the third house along the second block unless you have had reason to bring your PSA to the paint colour. On your walk you have only paid peripheral or ambient attention. Similarly, when you have a vigorous conversation with another person your PSA is between yourself and the other person, where you focus intently on their face, their expressions and the content of the conversation. Yet while you are having that conversation, you have some peripheral awareness for things going on around you, such as noises or objects in the vicinity or fleeting thoughts or images. This peripheral or ambient attention has been shown to be lost from memory fairly rapidly and is probably not consolidated to LTM. On the other hand, PSA results in the synchronous firing that promotes dendritic spine proliferation and synaptic consolidation, protein synthesis and LTM formation. In this way, a person can still have ambient awareness of their well-practised anxiety mentations without bringing them into their focussed attention. People are not asked to *get rid* of their anxiety mentations merely to not pay them any focussed attention.

CONCLUSION

ST aims to provide a simple and coherent explanation that is supported by contemporary neuroscience research about how transient anxiety symptoms related to SLEs and the subsequent increase in CRF effects of brain agitation and hyper-vigilance, can transform into a persistent anxiety 'disorder' due to PSA activating *normal* learning and LTM consolidation through the proliferation and stabilisation of dendritic spines and the strengthening of related neural circuitry over time due to increased synaptic traffic. This approach makes sense of the fact that anxious people do consistently show increased CRF levels but that they do not consistently exhibit any other neural pathology. From this perspective we are able to identify why some people who are more *threat-ready* because they have already had higher levels of objective threat in their background, respond to the threat of SLEs with higher levels of PSA than do those who have had fewer experiences of objective threat and are therefore less *threat-ready*. Since the precise underlying neurological mechanisms that trigger and then maintain anxiety are able to be identified then we are able to be equally precise in outlining the exact treatment for anxiety.

REFERENCES

Andrews, G., Hall, W., Teesson, M., & Henderson, S. (1999). *The Mental Health of Australians.* Canberra, ACT: Commonwealth of Australia.

Alvarez, V.A., & Sabatini, B. (2007). 'Anatomical and Physiological Plasticity of Dendritic Spines', *Annual Review of Neuroscience,* 30, 79–97.

American Psychiatric Association (2000). *Diagnostic and Statistical Manual of Mental Disorders,* 4th edn., Text Revision. Washington, DC, American Psychiatric Association.

American Psychiatric Association (2013). *Diagnostic and Statistical Manual of Mental Disorders,* 5h edn. Washington, DC, American Psychiatric Association.

Awh, E., Vogel, E.K., & Oh, S.H. (2006). 'Interactions Between Attention and Working Memory', *Neuroscience, 139*(1), 201–8.

Baddeley, A.D., & Hitch, G.J. (1974). 'Working memory', G.A. Bower (ed.), *The Psychology of Learning and Motivation.* New York, NY: Academic Press, 47–89.

Baddeley, A.D. (2000). 'The Episodic Buffer: A New Component of Working Memory?', *Trends in Cognitive Sciences,* 4(11), 417–23.

Beck, A.T., Emery, G.E. &, Greenberg, R.L. (2005). *Anxiety Disorders and Phobias – A Cognitive Perspective.* New York, NY: Basic Books, Harper & Row Ltd.

Belloch, A., Morillo, C., Luciano, J.V., Garcia-Soriano, G., Cabedo, E., & Carrio, C. (2010). 'Dysfunctional Belief Domains Related to Obsessive-Compulsive Disorder: A Further Examination of Their Dimensionality and Specificity', *The Spanish Journal of Psychology,* 13(1), 376–88.

Blank, T., & Spiess, J. (2009). 'Corticotropin-Releasing Factor (CRF) and CRF-Related Peptides – A Linkage Between Stress and Anxiety, in Stress', H. Soreq, A. Friedman & D. Kaufer (eds.) *From Molecules to Behavior: A Comprehensive Analysis of the Neurobiology of Stress Responses.* Germany: Wiley.

Buffalo E.A., Fries, P., Landman, R., Liang, H., & Desimone, R. (2010). 'A Backward Progression of Attentional Effects in the Ventral Stream', *Proceedings of the National Academy of Sciences,* 107(1), 361–5.

Bunge, S.A., Ochsner, K.N., Desmond, J.E., Glover, G.H., & Gabrieli, J.D.E. (2001). 'Prefrontal Regions Involved in Keeping Information in and out of Mind', *Brain,* 124, 2074–86.

Calabrese, B; Wilson, M.S., & Halpain, S. (2006). 'Development and Regulation of Dendritic Spine Synapses', *Physiology*, 21(1), 38–47.

Chun, M.M. & Turk-Browne, N.B. (2007). 'Interactions Between Attention and Memory', *Cognitive Neuroscience*, 17(2), 177–84.

Constantinidis, C., & Goldman-Rakic, P.S. (2002). 'Correlated Discharges Among Putative Pyramidal Neurons and Interneurons in the Primate Prefrontal Cortex', *Journal of Neurophysiology*, 88(6), 3487–97.

Cook, C.J. (2004). 'Stress Induces CRF Release in the Paraventicular Nucleus, and Both CRF and GABA Release in the Amygdala', *Physiology & Behavior*, 82(4), 751–62.

Dorin, R.I., Zlock, D.W., & Kilpatrick, K. (1993). 'Transcriptional Regulation of Human Corticotrophin Releasing Factor Gene Expression by Cyclic Adenosine 3',5'-Monophosphate: Differential Effects at Proximal and Distal Promoter Elements', *Molecular Cell Endocrinology*, 96(1–2), 99–111.

Dunn, A.J., & Berridge, C.W. (1990). 'Physiological and Behavioural Responses to Corticotrophin-Releasing Factor Administration: Is CRF a Mediator of Anxiety or Stress Responses?', *Brain Research Reviews*, 15, 71–100.

Eifert, G.H., & Forsyth, J.P. (2005). 'Controlling Anxiety is the Problem, not a Solution', *Acceptance and Commitment Therapy for Anxiety Disorders*. Oakland, Canada: New Harbinger Publications Inclusive, 47–67.

Evans, J., Xu, K., Heron, J., Enoch, M.A., Araya, R., Lewis, G., Timpson, N., Davies, S., Nutt, D., & Goldman, D. (2009). 'Emotional Symptoms in Children: The Effect of Maternal Depression, Life Events, and COMT Genotype', *American Journal of Medical Genetics Part B: Neuropsychiatric Genetics*, 150B, 209–18.

Fredman, S., Hirshfeld-Becker, D., Smoller, J. & Rosenbaum, J. (2007). 'Childhood Antecedents of Adult Anxiety Disorders', D. Nutt & J. Ballenger (eds.) *Anxiety Disorders*. Oxford, UK: Blackwell Science Ltd.

Fries, P., Reynolds, J.H., Rorie, A.E. & Desimone, R. (2001). 'Modulation of Oscillatory Neuronal Synchronization by Selective Visual Attention', *Science*, 291, 1560–3.

Fu, M., Yu, X., Lu, J. & Zuo, Y. (2012). 'Repetitive Motor Learning Induces Coordinated Formation of Clustered Dendritic Spines in Vivo', *Nature*, 483(7387), 92–5.

Gregoriou, G.G., Gotts, S.J., Zhou, H. & Desimone, R. (2009). 'High-Frequency, Long-Range Coupling Between Prefrontal and Visual Cortex During Attention', *Science*, 324, 1207–10.

Harvey, C.D. & Svoboda, K. (2007). 'Locally Dynamic Synaptic Learning Rules in Pyramidal Neuron Dendrites', *Nature*, 450, 1195–200.

Hauger, R.L., Risbrough, V., Oakley, R.H., Olivares-Reyes, J.A. & Dautzenberg, F.M. (2009). 'Role of CRF Receptor Signalling in Stress Vulnerability, Anxiety and Depression', *Annals of the New York Academy of Sciences*, 1179, 120–43.

Hayes, S.C., & Strosahl, K.D. (eds.) (2004). *A practical guide to Acceptance and Commitment Therapy*. New York: Springer-Verlag.

Hettema, J.M., Prescott, C.A., Kendler, K.S. (2004). 'Genetic and Environmental Sources of Covariation Between Generalized Anxiety Disorder and Neuroticism', *The American Journal of Psychiatry*, 161(9), 1581–7.

Hicks, B.M., DiRago, A.C., Iacono, W.G., & McGue, M. (2009). 'Gene-Environment Interplay in Internalizing Disorders: Consistent Findings Across Six Environmental Risk Factors', *Journal of Child Psychology and Psychiatry*, 50(10), 1309–17.

Holsboer, F. (2000). 'The Corticosteroid Receptor Hypothesis of Depression', *Neuropsychopharmacology*, 23, 477–501.

Hopko, D.R.; Robertson, S. & Lejuez, C.W. (2006). 'Behavioral Activation for Anxiety Disorders', *The Behavior Analyst Today*, 7(2), 212–33.

Kandel, E.R. (2006). *In Search of Memory: The emergence of a new science of mind*. New York: W.W. Norton & Company.

Kaech, S., Brinkhaus, H. & Matus, A. (1999). 'Volatile Anesthetics Block Actin-Based Motility in Dendritic Spines', *Proceedings of the National Academy of Science (USA)*, 96, 10433–7.

Kasai, H., Fukuda, M., Watanabe, S., Hayashi-Takagi, A. & Noguchi, J. (2010). 'Structural Dynamics of Dendritic Spines in Memory and Cognition', *Trends in Neurosciences*, 33(3), 121–9.

Kasai, H., Matsuzaki, M., Noguchi, J., Yasumatsu, N. & Nakahara, H. (2003). 'Structure-Stability-Function Relationships of Dendritic Spines', *Trends in Neurosciences*, 26(7), 360–8.

Kastner, S., De Weerd, P., Desimone, R. & Ungerleider, L.G. (1998). 'Mechanisms of Directed Attention in the Human Extrastriate Cortex as Revealed by Functional MRI', *Science*, 282, 108–11.

Keane, T. & Barlow, D.H. (2002). 'Posttraumatic Stress Disorder', David H. Barlow (ed.) *Anxiety and Its Disorders: The Nature and Treatment of Anxiety and Panic*, 2nd edn. New York: The Guilford Press.

Kendler, K.S., Walters, E.E., Neale, M.C., Kessler, R.C., Heath, A.C. & Eaves, L.J. (1995). 'The Structure of the Genetic and Environmental Risk Factors for Six Major Psychiatric Disorders in Women', *Archives of General Psychiatry*, 52(5), 374–83.

Kentros, C.G., Agnihotri, N.T., Streater, S., Hawkins, R.D. & Kandel, E.R. (2004). 'Increased Attention to Spatial Context Increases Both Place Field Stability and Spatial Memory', *Neuron*, 42, 283–95.

Klauke, B., Deckert, J., Reif, A., Pauli, P. & Domschke, K. (2010). 'Life Events in Panic Disorder – An Update on "Candidate Stressors"', *Depression and Anxiety*, 27, 716–30.

Kondo, H., Osaka, N. & Osaka, M. (2004). 'Cooperation of the Anterior Cingulated Cortex and Dorsolateral Prefrontal Cortex for Attention Shifting', *NeuroImage*, 23, 670–9.

Lesscher, H.M.B., McMahon, T., Lasek, A.W., Chou, W.H., Connoly, J., Kharazia, V. & Messing, R.O. (2008). 'Amygdala Protein Kinase C Epsilon Regulates Corticiptropin-Releasing Factor and Anxiety-Like Behavior', *Genes, Brain and Behavior*, 7, 323–33.

Lewis, M.W., Hermann, G.E., Rogers, R.C., & Travagli, R.A. (2002). 'In Vitro and In Vivo Analysis of the Effects of Corticotrophin Releasing Factor on Rat Dorsal Vagal Complex', *The Journal of Physiology*, 543, 135–46.

Linthorst, A.C.E., Penalva, R.G., Flachskamm, Cl, Holsboer, F., & Reul, J. (2002). 'Forced Swim Stress Activates Rat Hippocampal Serotonergic Neurotransmission Involving a Corticotrophin-Releasing Hormone Receptor-Dependent Mechanism', *European Journal of Neuroscience*, 16, 2441–52.

Lowry, C.A., Rodda, J.E., Lightman, S.L., Ingram, C.D. (2000). 'Corticotropin-Releasing Factor Increases In Vitro Firing Rates of Serotonergic Neurons in the Rat Dorsal Raphe Nucleus: Evidence for Activation of a Topographically Organised Mesolimbocortical Serotonergic System', *Journal of Neuroscience*, 20, 7728–36.

Luciano, J.V. & Gonzalez, S.A. (2007). 'Analysis of the Efficacy of different Thought Suppression Strategies', *International Journal of Psychology and Psychological Therapy*, 7(3), 335–45.

Matsuo, N., Reijmers, L. & Mayford, M. (2008). 'Spine-Type Specific Recruitment of Newly Synthesized AMPA Receptors with Learning', *Science*, 319, 1104–7.

Matsuzaki, M., Honkura, N., Ellis-Davies, G.C. & Kasai, H. (2004). 'Structural Basis of Long-Term Potentiation in Single Dendritic Spines', *Nature*, 429, 761–6.

Medalla, M. & Barbas, H. (2009). 'Synapses with Inhibitory Neurons Differentiate Anterior Cingulated from Dorsolateral Prefrontal Pathways Associated with Cognitive Control', *Neuron*, 61(4), 609–20.

Merali, Z., Anisman, H., James, J.S., Kent, P. & Schulkin, J. (2008). 'Effects of Corticosterone on Corticotrophin-Releasing Hormone and Gastrin-Releasing Peptide Release in Response to an Aversive Stimulus in Two Regions of the Forebrain (Central Nucleus of the Amygdale and Prefrontal Cortex)', *European Journal of Neuroscience*, 28, 165–72.

Nagerl, U.V., Eberhorn, N., Cambridge, S.B. & Bonhoeffer, T. (2004). 'Bidirectional Activity-Dependent Morphological Plasticity in Hippocampal Neurons', *Neuron*, 44 (5), 759–67.

Niebur, E., Hsiao, S.S. & Johnson, K.O. (2002). 'Synchrony: A Neuronal Mechanism for Attentional Selection', *Current Opinion in Neurobiology*, 12, 190–4.

Ostroff, L.E., Cain, C.K., Bedont, J., Monfils, M.H. & LeDoux, J.F. (2010). 'Fear and Safety Learning Differentially Affect Synapse Size and Dendritic Translation in the Lateral Amygdale', *Proceedings of the National Academy of Sciences*, 107(20), 9418–23.

Owens, M.J. and Nemeroff, C.B. (2007). 'The Role of Corticotropin-Releasing Factor in the Pathophysiology of Affective and Anxiety Disorders: Laboratory and Clinical Studies', D.J. Chadwick, J. Marsh and K. Ackrill (eds.) *Corticotropin-Releasing Factor*. Chichester, UK: John Wiley & Sons, Ltd.,

Page, M.E. & Abercrombie, E.D. (1999). 'Discrete Local Application of Corticotrophin-Releasing Factor Increases Locus Coeruleus Discharge and Extracellular Norepinephrine in Rat Hippocampus', *Synapase*, 33, 304–13.

Peeters, P., Moechars, D., Grohlmann, H., Swagemakers, S., Kass, S., Langlois, X., Stenzel-Poore, M., Bakker, M. & Steckler, T. (2002). 'Gene Expression Profiling of CRF Signalling', *Society for Neuroscience Abstracts*, 28, 222–3.

Purdon, C. & Clark, D.A. (2001). 'Suppression of Obsession-Like Thoughts in Nonclinical Individuals: Impact on Thought Frequency, Appraisal and Mood State', *Behaviour Research and Therapy*, 39, 1163–81.

Restivo, L., Vetere, G., Bontempi, B. & Ammassari-Teule, M. (2009). 'The Formation of Recent and Remote Memory is Associated with Time-Dependent Formation of Dendritic Spines in the Hippocampus and Anterior Cingulated Cortex', *Journal of Neuroscience*, 29(25), 8206–14.

Roberts, Tl, Tschida, K., Klein, M. & Mooney, R. (2010). 'Rapid Spine Stabilization and Synaptic Enhancement at the Onset of Behavioural Learning', *Nature*, 463, 948–52.

Salkovskis, P.M. & Campbell, P. (1994). 'Thought Suppression Induces Intrusion in Naturally Occurring Negative Intrusive Thoughts', *Behaviour Research and Therapy*, 32(1), 1–8.

Salkovskis, P.M., Wroe, A.L., Gledhill, A., Morrison, N., Forrester, E., Richards, C., Reynolds, M. & Thorpe, S. (2000). 'Responsibility Attitudes and Interpretations are Characteristic of Obsessive Compulsive Disorder', *Behaviour Research and Therapy*, 38(4), 347–72.

Sakamoto, K., Mushiake, H., Saito, N., Aihara, K., Yano, M. & Tanji, J. (2008). 'Discharge Synchrony During the Transition of Behavioural Goal Representations Encoded by Discharge Rates of Prefrontal Neurons', *Cerebral Cortex*, 18(9), 2036–45.

Sandi, C., Cordero, M.I., Ugolini, A., Varea, E., Caberiotto, L. & Large, C.H. (2008). 'Chronic Stress-Induced Alterations in Amygdale Responsiveness and Behaviour – Modulation by Trait Anxiety and Corticotrophin-Releasing Factor Systems', *European Journal of Neuroscience*, 28, 1836–48.

Schildkraut, J.J. (1965). 'The Catecholamine Hypothesis of Affective Disorders: A Review of Supporting Evidence', *American Journal of Psychiatry*, 122, 509–22.

Shekhar, A., Truitt, W., Rainnie, D. & Sajdyk, T. (2005). 'Role of stress, Corticotrophin Releasing Factor (CRF) and Amygdala Plasticity in Chronic Anxiety', *Informa Healthcare*, 8(4), 209–19.

Steinmetz, P.N., Roy, A., Fitzgerald, P.J., Hsiao, S.S., Johnson, K.O. & Niebur, E. (2000). 'Attention Modulates Synchronized Neuronal Firing in Primate Somatosensory Cortex', *Nature*, 404, 187–90.

Tanaka, J., Horiike, Y., Matsuzaki, M., Miyazaki, T. Ellis-Davies, G.C.R. & Kasai, H. (2008). 'Protein Synthesis and Neurotrophin-Dependent Structural Plasticity of Single Dendritic Spines', *Science*, 319, 1683–7.

Thompson, B.L., Erickson, K., Schulkin, J.& Rosen, J.B. (2004). 'Corticosterone Facilitates Retention of Contextually Conditioned Fear and Increases CRH mRNA Expression in the Amygdale', *Behavioural Brain Research*, 149, 209–15.

Todorovic, C., Radulovic, J., Jahn, O., Radulovic, M., Sherrin, T., Hippel, C. & Spiess, J. (2007). 'Differential Activation of CRF Receptor Subtypes Removes Stress-Induced Memory Deficit and Anxiety', *European Journal of Neuroscience*, 25, 3385–97.

Tolin, D.F, Abramowitz, J.S., Przeworski, A. & Foa, E.B. (2002). 'Thought Suppression in Obsessive-Compulsive Disorder', *Behaviour Research and Therapy*, 40(11), 1255–74.

Tootell, R.B.H. & Hadjikhami, N. (2000). 'Attention – Brains at Work!', *Nature Neuroscience*, 3(3), 206–8.

Ure, J., Videla, H. & Ollari, J. (2009). 'Neuroanatomy of Consciousness'. Online publication: www.scitopics.com.

Wegner, D.M., Schneider, D.J., Carter, S. & White, T. (1987). 'Paradoxical Effects of Thought Suppression', *Journal of Personality and Social Psychology*, 53, 5–13.

Whittal, M.L. & McLean, P.D. (1999). 'CBT for OCD: The Rationale, Protocol, and Challenges', *Cognitive and Behavioral Practice*, 6(4), 383–96.

Yang, G., Pan, F. & Gan, W.B. (2009). 'Stably Maintained Dendritic Spines are Associated with Lifelong Memories', *Nature*, 462, 920–24.

Yuste, R. (2010). *Dendritic Spines*. Cambridge, Massachusetts: The MIT Press.

Zhou, Q., Homma, K.J., & Poo, M. (2004). 'Shrinkage of Dendritic Spines Associated with Long-Term Depression of Hippocampal Synapses', *Neuron*, 44, 749–57.

www.ingramcontent.com/pod-product-compliance
Lightning Source LLC
Chambersburg PA
CBHW030853170426
43193CB00009BA/594